CHINA
DEVELOPING

Cultural Identity of Emerging Societies

CHINA
DEVELOPING

Cultural Identity of Emerging Societies

George Fusun Ling
D. Phil. Oxford

 **World Scientific**

NEW JERSEY · LONDON · SINGAPORE · BEIJING · SHANGHAI · HONG KONG · TAIPEI · CHENNAI

Published by

World Scientific Publishing Co. Pte. Ltd.

5 Toh Tuck Link, Singapore 596224

USA office: 27 Warren Street, Suite 401-402, Hackensack, NJ 07601

UK office: 57 Shelton Street, Covent Garden, London WC2H 9HE

Library of Congress Cataloging-in-Publication Data
Ling, George Fusun.
   China developing : cultural identity of emerging societies / George Fusun Ling.
     p. cm.
   Includes bibliographical references and index.
   ISBN 978-981-277-863-5
   ISBN 978-981-283-590-1 (pbk)
   1. Political culture--China. I. Title.
   JQ1516.L52 2008
   323.0951--dc22

                                             2007034289

British Library Cataloguing-in-Publication Data
A catalogue record for this book is available from the British Library.

Typeset by Stallion Press
Email: enquiries@stallionpress.com

Printed in Singapore.

To Jennie, who has walked with me through the grimmest shadow of dark valleys as well as over the sunny slopes of high mountains to behold the horizon of our destiny. Walking with us also are Cedric, Kristina and Derek who might not have been with the troupe at all times, but have never been absent from our caring thoughts and the deepest part of our hearts

Preface

This book comes at the end of my prolonged reflection on events that have puzzled me intellectually for many years. Being a fourth generation Chinese studying in America and England, I have come to understand and respect many deep-seated ideas and values upheld in the West and promoted by the West to the rest of the world in the past 200 or so years. And yet, as I looked back on Asian history of the last 50 years, I was continually puzzled by how unsuccessful those values and ideas had played out socioeconomically as well as culturally in some of the developing countries.

In the meantime, after my studies in Oberlin College, U.C. Berkeley, Yale, and Oxford Universities, I came to China together with my family to live through 9 out of the 10 years of the Cultural Revolution. And later I came to China again as a businessman to witness the development of China under the open-door policy over the last 28 years or so. Those experiences gave me a rare opportunity to witness first-hand how some Western values have and have not played out well in contemporary China.

After observing 50 years of Asian history, I have discovered that, although socioeconomic and political systems are important to a country in their own rights, understanding of cultural values undergirding the systems are of even more critical importance for developing countries. This book is an attempt to find a way to deal with this intellectual search. Globalization today has brought insecurities to many third-world countries, though China has benefited from it economically. But all developing countries, including China, are faced with a search for cultural identity especially when they are drawn into the forceful waves and tricky undercurrents of globalization. Our world today may be deeply interconnected technologically, economically, and culturally, and is unavoidably interactive politically. But the sovereignty and dignity of some developing countries are being challenged. Therefore, how to find cultural identity under such circumstances becomes vitally important for developing countries today.

World affairs are often determined by power politics with self-interests of the powers, and not so much by philosophical ideas and moral values. On the other hand, when leaders of developing countries want to plot directions, establish institutions for their societies, and improve the welfare, confidence, and dignity of their people, they have to base their visions and planning upon concepts and values that would be beneficial to their countries and their people. Ultimately, in other words, all important decisions such as those about the constitution, political system, socioeconomic institutions, and legal system of a country will have to be based upon deep-seated and most cherished values of that culture in order for the development to be meaningful to the people of that country.

My attempt is to suggest an approach to understand, and to deal with, a few important concepts in sociopolitical philosophy for a contemporary modern society in one's cultural context while implementing them in one's historical context. The approach may be carried out in such a way that those concepts could be accepted as the meaningful and dominant tools for development in those countries. For discussion in this book, I have selected the following prevalent concepts as important: respect for the individual person, human rights, freedom, equality, democracy, and the universal respect for law. My suggestion is that we have to do two things: One is to analyze the concepts to understand their nuances; secondly, to have an honest look at one's own culture to find what are its deep-seated and most cherished values.

I do not pretend to have knowledge of all cultures and their possible interpretations of the various concepts to suggest a model of development. My attempt is only to suggest a method of dealing with those development intellectually, so that potential leaders of developing countries could use the methodology to assist their thinking on some of the important concepts in relation to their own national development. And other readers may use it to understand more thoroughly the concerns of developing countries. Due to my familiarity with China, I shall use perspectives in Chinese culture and events in Chinese history as examples, and only as examples, in this book.

Although this book does not speak directly to the problems of indignation, hatred, violence, and unnecessary bloodshed that are so widespread in the world today, it is dedicated to those committed to work toward the elimination of poverty, ignorance, physical miseries as well as national humiliation, in order to establish decency, dignity, order, hope, and ecologically sustainable prosperity, in the underdeveloped, as well as in the developing countries.

LING Fusun, George
2007

Preface to the Paperback Edition

So much relating to developing countries have happened since the final proof of the hardcover edition of my book in late 2006, that I feel it necessary to say a few words here to elucidate or emphasize certain points.

First, China's GDP has continued to grow at a two-digit pace since China's RMB appreciated around 20% against the USD between July, 2005 and June, 2008.

Second, China's economy has merely been slightly affected while facing the world-wide economic slowdown. Russia's economy has also thrived under non-Western style democracy. The above events indicate again that economic vitality is not necessarily related to Western style democracies in emerging societies.

Third, the effects of globalization have further worsened recently in certain aspects; such as the global food shortage crisis. Worse-hit by the crisis are the world's "have-nots". And the oil price rising out of control is even hurting the masses of some oil producing countries, like Nigeria, where there is no refined oil at home for small businessmen who have to buy petroleum on the world market at the sky-rocketing market price.

Fourth, an advocate of strong (not dictatorial) governments in emerging societies, Prof. Lin Yifu (林毅夫) from China, has been appointed to be the chief economist and senior vice president of the World Bank. This indicates that the World Bank is taking a serious look at emerging societies having strong governments, though the unknown factor is whether the chief economist will change World Bank's neoliberalism philosophy or he himself not survive his post there.

Five, two historic calamities have recently happened almost simultaneously in two countries, Myanmar and China, both with a single party political system and both without universal election in their systems. However, the swiftness of response in relief work, the accountability shown in the leadership, the transparency in international media coverage as well as in seeking international relief expertise, and the spontaneous out-pouring of popular compassion displayed in volunteering work and donations have been entirely different in these two countries. This again indicates the theme of the book; namely, cultural and social values undergirding the politico-socio-economic systems are just as significant and important as the structure and mechanism of the systems themselves.

Acknowledgment

It is difficult to acknowledge all the people from whom I have benefited in a book that reflects over 50 years of experience and observation. However, directly related to this book, I am grateful to Prof. Lee H. Yearley of Stanford University who has given me encouragement from the inception of the project and later, valuable comments on the whole book. I am grateful to Prof. Gene Outka of Yale University for his insightful comments and helpful suggestions on sections of the book. I am also deeply grateful to Prof. Barbara Harris-White of Oxford University, who shared her insight into political economy and gave me the most valuable comments and suggestions. Dr. Maria Jaschok of Oxford University had given me direction in the early stage of the book. To all of them I am indebted for their interest, concern and contributions to the writing of this book, though of course, any remaining mistakes, misrepresentations and controversial points of view are all mine. Appreciation also goes to my wife for her meticulous proofreading.

George F. Ling

Contents

Introduction

After 11 September 2001 many people are asking the question: what sort of desperation drove supposedly intelligent young men and woman to take such cruel, horrible, and ghastly action, and what terribly deep-seated hatred and hopelessness must they have to make them take a seemingly insensible suicidal option. And then the horrible bombing in the London underground on 7 July 2005, and many other bombings in crowded places all seem senseless. Whatever the motives, the mass killing of innocent people has no excuse. The whole ideology behind it must be understood then challenged, the network behind such plots must be checked and the inhumane acts themselves must be stopped.

On the other hand, it is also clear that the 9/11 and 7/7 (London bombing) events epitomized anti-Western sentiments such as the sabotage of American military and civilian targets in parts of the world, and recent opposition to the invasion of Iraq in many parts of the world. At first, it does not seem understandable why, despite what America has done to promote democracy and human rights, and to alleviate the plight of people in many under developed and developing countries around the world, that it is still bitterly hated by many. In Iraq, to take a recent example, America, together with its coalition partners, through the sacrifice of their soldiers, eliminated a dictator who was ruthless to a great majority of the Iraqi people. And yet in return, the American campaign in Iraq is not even appreciated by many Iraqis. The campaign is being understood and appreciated less and less as the months and years go by.

Somehow, as the titles of two books[1] have indicated, instead of planting democracy and providing hope for the people around the world, America is deterring democracy and killing hope. It is the right time to re-examine the worldwide human situation that produces terrorism and ways to deal with it, and also to rethink American foreign policy around the world in relation to the roots of Islamic fanatic terrorism in particular. And the examination has to be done in relation to the concept of American Empire[2] against the background of the powerlessness of people in many parts of the world. At the same time, developing countries themselves also need to find their own solutions. History requires us to rethink the ideas and institutions that the West has been exporting to developing countries in the 19th and 20th centuries and in more recent times. Dealing intellectually with such issues for the developing countries is, then, the primary concern of this book. In a division of labor, some have to strategize ways to deal with terrorism and suggest how American foreign policy can speak to those who are utterly hopeless, instead of flexing its muscles. Others have to provide intellectual alternative so that under developed countries could rise out of the ashes of identity annihilation due to cultural imperialism, and developing countries could emerge from the agony of birth pangs of modern capitalism, commercialism, and the reduction of the state to dealing with commodities without ideals. And it seems clear that for the under developed and the developing countries, this mission could only be accomplished through an awareness and a critical examination of some important concepts for contemporary modern societies and a country's own cultural identities.

---

[1] See Noam Chomsky, *Deterring Democracy*; William Blum, *Killing Hope*. These two references to American foreign policies were first given by David Ray Griffin in an unpublished work: *Shaping Christian Faith in an Age of Global Empire*.

[2] See Andrew Bacevich, *American Empire*; Also Noam Chomsky, *Failed States*.

In the discussion of this book, I am using the word "culture" in a very confined sense. Culture, in a broad sense, has been used to denote the total traces of human activities in a society, including its language, mores, religion, the arts and crafts vis-à-vis the geography, climate or ethnicity, etc. of that society. In a slightly narrower sense, "culture" has been used to denote a specific group of activities in a society, such as its literature, music, and the plastic, three-dimensional and performing arts, vis-à-vis the society's political, social, economic and legal systems and activities. In this book, however, when talking about culture in relation to cultural identity, I am using it as the undergirding strength of a society's communal psyche, historical memories, legends, myths, and its symbols of dignity and well-being that have all been reflected in a set of deep-seated and most cherished values. However, I have occasionally used culture in a broader sense, when I talk about a people's history and culture, or their cultural confrontation with other cultures, or in relations to other broadly based categories, like country, society, people, etc.

This book also deals with "modernization" of developing countries, but the term "modern" is ambiguous. For historians usually use that word to designate the industrial stage of development, and we are now in the information age. Although some developing countries are developing information technologies, these and the bulk of developing countries are still worrying about problems of industrialization. Thus in this book, I shall use "contemporary modern society" to indicate the stage of development that most developing countries wish to strive for today.

The cultural confusion of developing countries in Asia brought about by a confrontation with the West more than 2 centuries ago (earlier contacts might be dramatic, but not confusing) is today compounded by the onslaught of globalization in information technology, and in trade and finance with their economic, social, political, and cultural impacts. The flood of variegated information from the Internet and the dazzling foreign images delivered, especially, by movies and television media have become common phenomena in everyday life in developing countries. Likewise, global trading has brought foreign fashions, foreign vehicles, and multinational fast food and retail chains to the immediate availability of people in developing countries. What is more important for our discussion are the effects of globalization defined basically by the "Washington Consensus" under the economic theory of neo-liberalism. Globalization, in this sense, really started in the latter part of the 20th century, bringing about extremely large amount of trade and capital movements. This could and should have been a positive force for the development. But unfortunately, the financial assistance to developing countries by international financial institutions such as the World Bank and IMF (International Monetary Fund) often dictate the running of the recipient countries, including such requirements as limiting state power, privatizing enterprises, deregulating controls, and liberalizing the market by opening it up to world trading.[3] As Held and McGrew, quoting Pieper and Taylor, summarizes, "Today 50 percent of the world's population and two-thirds of its governments are bound by the disciplines of the IMF or the World Bank".[4]

No developing country objects to assistance in economic analysis and financial funding from such international institutions. What is daunting, especially to small and weak nations, is the indiscernible erosion of cultural identity and sovereignty of national power by their embedded cultural values and demands, as their dictates overpower the autonomy of those nations. And the requirement of opening up the markets of the smaller and weaker nations to worldwide competition has made them victims of the "survival of the fittest".

Putting aside the question, for the time being, of whether or not globalization has worsened poverty in the world, or whether it has increased the gap between rich and poor countries, it is definitely threatening the autonomy and sovereignty of the nation state; especially that of the smaller and weaker nations. According to Barbara Harris-White, globalization, by exposing the economies of all third-world countries to competition in production, price, wage,

---

[3] See Chris Brown, "A World Gone Wrong?" in *Global Transformation Reader*, p. 570.
[4] Held and McGrew, "Introduction" in *Ibid*, p. 30.

and taxation on the open market, has created insecurity for both people and their property in those countries, in terms of unemployment and asset loss; instability of local markets; and vulnerability of people's positions in work and social security.[5] Yet, for a country to be able to play a responsible role in this increasingly internationalized economy, there is precisely the need for it to be a capable and sovereign state. Manuel Castells observes: "The global economy was not created by markets, but by the interaction between markets and governments and international financial institutions acting on behalf of markets—or of their notion of what markets ought to be".[6] And it needs a sovereign state to redress the unevenness and injustice in the globalization process. Thus, in order for these states to have the confidence to act responsibly, it is vitally and extremely important today for each country to have cultural identity and national sovereignty.

In dealing with this question, the issue of East versus West has been with us for a long time. If the developing countries rejected what the West has imposed, then in what direction should they go? Historically, there have been two extreme reactions: a total acceptance of the West, or a total rejection of it on the ground of the West's world hegemony. The latter view, for instance, thinks that America's foreign policies are all about having a presence in strategic places around the world to guard America military; having friendly powers around to safeguard American interests politically; and gaining footholds in places rich in natural resources so that Americans gain the advantage economically.

The trouble with this reaction to America's hegemony is that, while the analysis might be very true, it only gives a negative criticism without providing a direction for developing countries themselves. Historically, many attempts at regime change failed because the protagonists did not have a political platform or ideas about workable socioeconomic institutions based on generally accepted values. The failures of many peasant rebellions in China are good

---

[5] See Barbara Harriss-White, *Globalization and Insecurity*, p. 3.
[6] "Global Informational Capitalism" in *The Global Transformations Reader*, p. 326.

examples.[7] And the terrorists today could be another example, though there are quite a bit of discussions and debates regarding possible muslim sociopolitical structures since 9/11. After venting their hatred, what direction will they offer to build their societies?

The trouble with the former reaction of total acceptance is that the values, ideas, and institutions promoted by the West could clash with deep-seated indigenous cultural values, and become irrelevant to the local conditions and people. Going back a hundred years or so, we see similar problems of confrontation that China faced in the late 19th and early 20th centuries. After the humiliating impact of Western powers, China went through the biggest peasant movement in its history, the Taiping Rebellion, which attempted to integrate some of the Western, especially Christian ideas, into traditional thinking. It was followed by the 100-Day Reform of Kang Yuwei, and the cultural reforms of Liang Qichao and Yan Fu,[8] to eradicate feudal institutions like footbinding of women and to start modern education for women and Li Hongzhang (1823–1901) with his industrial and military modernization programs. While all these reforms were taking place, the feudal habit of thinking was still binding, especially when China lost a sea battle against another Asian country, Japan, in 1898. That experience gave China a huge blow, because it indicated that China still had a long way to go for modernization.

In 1911, the revolution by Sun Yat-sen overthrew the feudal imperial system in China. But it did not eradicate the plight of warlordism throughout the country. Then, intellectuals like Chen Duxiu and Hu Shi, concluding what China lacked was a modern culture, started to criticize the Confucian tradition and wanted to introduce modern science and Western democracy among intellectual circles. This "new thought movement", which began with the publication of the journal *La Jeunesse* in 1917,[9] inspired an intellectual movement

---

[7] See J.A.G. Roberts, *A History of China* Vol I, pp. 177–180 (The success of one of the peasant rebels, Zu Yuan-zhang who eventually became the emperor of the Ming dynasty, was made possible because he allied with the local gentry and military leaders for political ideas and administrative wisdom).

[8] See Ye Nanrong, (叶南容), *Modernization of China* (中国的现代化), pp. 45–59.

[9] See *Ibid*, p. 62ff.

which led the students to stage a mass demonstration on 4 May 1919 against the government's earlier weakness in agreeing to the Twenty-One Demands by Japan in 1915 and the current weakness against the Western dictates in the Treaties of Versailles in 1919. Both incidents were humiliating to China as a sovereign nation. The movement was later immortalized as the May Fourth Spirit. At that time, while many students and intellectuals embraced the fresh ideas of modern science and Western democracy, China as a whole did not do so, because the new concepts clashed with the basic spirit of China's traditional ideas and institutions, and more importantly, they did not alleviate the plight of the vast majority of the Chinese people at the time: the rural peasant population. At a later date, however, a Chinese version of Marxism as propounded by Mao Zedong[10] spoke to the peasants' problems. Also, the ideal of ultimate equality among all peoples in Marxism caught the imagination of many intellectuals, as it resonated with the Chinese concept of "The Grand Harmony"[11] which was the basis of Kang Yuwei's book, *Da Tong Shu* (大同书). Part of that ideal came from a document probably written between 551 and 479 BC called Li Yun from the *Book of Poetry*. It said that in the days when there was grand harmony in the world:

> "...The great Dao was in practice. The world was common to all; those who were righteous and capable were selected to manage the affairs of the society; trust and peace were emphasized, so that people did not merely love their own parents and their own children. The aged were provided for; adults could each contribute according to his ability; children had healthy development; the widowers, widows, orphans, and those who were lonely and disabled all had their security. Men had employment and women had safety. They hated to see that natural resources be left untapped or used only by themselves, and that labor did not come from oneself or was only for one's profit. In this way, intrigues and dark plotting naturally did not have a chance to develop. Thieves and robbers had no

---

[10] *Selected Works of Mao Tse-Tung* Vol. II, pp. 541–542; 634–636.
[11] Levenson, Joseph, "Marxism and the Middle Kingdom" in *Modern China*, pp. 229–236.

opportunity to be active. Consequently, at night one could sleep without shutting the door. It is called "Grand Harmony". [translation adapted by author] [12]

So the Communist movement in China spread rapidly in the rural areas with their land-redistributing program taking care of the poor and destitute peasants. The students and intellectuals in general, sympathizing with Marxism for its affinity with the ideals of grand harmony and universal equality, became the driving force in the cities. In this way, the army of the Communist Party was able to enlarge its influence, and later during the civil war (1947–1949) between the Communist and the Kuomingtong (KMT), the Communist army could move from victory to victory because the general masses were behind it. The motivating force came from a reform welcomed by the general populace and an ideology that found roots in the deep-seated and most cherished values in the Chinese culture.

This Chinese experience showed that, first of all, a society in its development has to build upon ideals that are rooted in deep-seated and most cherished values of its culture. Secondly, merely solving the problems of the social or economic elite in a society without alleviating the plight of the general masses does not answer the crucial questions of development, because it does not have the general populace behind it to make it a country-wide movement.

Of course in actuality, the process of modernization in China was more complex. Many combinations of programs and ideas had been tried and failed. For example, the attempt of combining traditional philosophy as the essence of beliefs with Western science and technology in matters of practicality propounded by Zhang Zhidong (张之洞) did not work, because China soon found that Western science and technology also carried with them beliefs and philosophical ideas, and that they were in conflict with Chinese traditional

---

[12] See Kang Youwei's 大同书, in *Ta T'ung Shu: The One World Philosophy of K'ang Yu Weis*, translated by Thompson and Laurence pp. 28–29 for Kang's reference to alledged Confucius' writing, "Li Yun" (礼运); Also see Chinese original in Feng, Yu-lan, *A Short History of Chinese Philosophy*, p. 174.

views. All in all, the whole problem of modernization has plagued Chinese intellectuals for more than the last hundred years. Even after the Communist Party succeeded in the revolution and established a new China in 1949, the different experiments of modernization still went on. Except for the first 7 years of solid development after 1949, none of the experiments, which included the tumultuous cultural revolution, seemed to have resulted in sustained improvement until Deng Xiaoping initiated the open-door policy in 1978/1979. That first movement pushed forward drastic economic reforms and then more recently, political reforms and social reforms while interacting with the world community. So, not until then did we see that China has latched onto something that might lead to a satisfactory and sustainable, albeit arduous, path toward a healthy development of a contemporary modern state. It has been a very long and tortuous journey. The purpose of this book, then, is my attempt to see if there is any way the modernization of other developing countries could be a shorter and less painful one.

My basic premise in this book is that concepts like respect for the individual person, human rights, freedom, equality, democracy, and the universal respect for law should be the minimum guides to a contemporary modern society. Therefore, they are important as a nominal framework for our discussion. Yin Baoyun's book on *Universal Crisis of Modernization* touches on those concepts, though that book's emphasis is on the developmental model of socio-economic and political structures, and is not directly related to the cultural values studied in this book. On the other hand, the socio-political ideas selected by him to characterize modernity in his book *What is Modernization* coincide with the list of concepts I have selected above, though presented in a slightly different way.[13] However, I shall show that, while taking those concepts as important, we need to dissect and examine them critically to understand the nuances of their meanings, and also need to understand them in each cultural context, and then use them in the unique historical context of each developing country. The tendency of people dealing with

---

[13] Yin Baoyun, *What is Modernization* (什么是现代化), p. 8.

modernization of developing countries, aside from total acceptance or total rejection of Western values, is often trying to find Western values in traditional heritage, or trying to read Western-values into traditional concepts. But we have already seen that in the development of some Asian countries, like China, neither holding on to traditional ways nor complete Westernization nor any superficial mixture of them have played out well in history. Take Western-style democracy for example. Although it worked out well in Japan under American tutelage after WWII, South Korea under democracy had its ups and downs, and made its highest economic growth when the country was under a centralized form of representative government. The Chaebols, though private, were under the government discipline. And the economic system was a tightly controlled one till the early 1990s.[14] India has had Western style democracy for almost 60 years, and yet until recently, it has not done much in eliminating abject poverty. The Philippines have yet to solve much of their poverty problems also after close to 60 years of democratic rule.

That is why I think, for example, to deal with modernization of China by merely studying Confucianism, analyzing and evaluating the solutions of the "traditionalist" (or the neo-traditionalist) and the "modernists" or even the "New Age" view, as Tamney and Chiang have done, is still caught in the dichotomy of East and West,[15] and will invariably end in a cul-de-sac. As early as 1940 Mao Zedong essentially said that whatever was useful, China would adopt, even though it might be from the West. And whatever was harmful, China should discard, even though it might be traditional Chinese.[16] Actually, Tamney and Chiang, in discussing modernization and Confucianism, also say that, "What is needed from intellectuals is

---

[14] See Chang Zheng (畅征), and Liu Qingjiang (刘青建), *General Discussion on Developing Countries' Politics and Economy* (发展中国家政治经济 概论), pp. 147–148; See also "Interpreting the Korean Crisis: Financial Liberalization, Industrial Policy and Corporate Governance" in *Financial Liberalization and the Asian Crisis*. Chang *et al*. (ed.), pp. 140–153.

[15] *Modernization, Globalization and Confucianism in Chinese Society* See especially, pp. 187–207.

[16] *Selected Works of Mao Tse-Tung* Vol. II, p. 707.

not lists of negatives, or even lists of positives and negatives, but judgments as to whether the benefits of modernization do or do not outweigh the cost".[17] The trouble is that we can know "what is useful and harmful", or "what is beneficial and costly" only after a passage of time, with historical hindsight. We need to have criteria to make decisions and to evaluate the historical outcome and not to decide arbitrarily. For instance, it should not be, as some people would say, that as long as a country has adopted Western-style democracy, irrespective of its ability or inability to solve its people's poverty or other socioeconomic and cultural problems, it should nevertheless be applauded, as if democracy is an end in itself.

We have seen that Western-style democracy has not been successful in building some Asian countries after decades of practice. Thus, in dealing with the cultural concerns of developing countries in this book, I am trying to throw off the yoke of the East/West dichotomy. And in its stead I suggest that we should first analyze those prevalently considered important sociopolitical concepts indicated above, and then have an honest look at the total cultural heritage of one's own country, identifying its deep-seated and most cherished values (cultural identity), and use them as resources to evaluate and understand those concepts. At the same time, the cultural identity, together with basic human subsistence requirements, will be used as the criteria for evaluating the historical outcome of decisions taken for development.

In using a country's cultural identity as resources to understand those concepts relating to development, if one finds that an important concept was never there in one's heritage, then one should adopt it gracefully. One might find cases whereby one's own cultural insight gives a variation on the usual understanding of a concept could make it more relevant to one's society, then one should treasure it. Or one might find discarded or buried values in one's culture could be significant to the much commercialized and spiritually hollow contemporary world, then one should revive and promote them. Or one might discover the values that have demonstrated the

---

[17] *Modernization, Globalization and Confucianism in Chinese Societies*, pp. 57–58.

resilience of one's history are also basic to the flourishing of the human spirit generally, and then one should recommend them.

Coming back to the stated prevalent concepts, I will first use them as a nominal framework for discussion. That is, those concepts will not be taken at face value, but be critically examined. They are selected, because they seem to represent the minimum characteristics of modernity, and due to that importance, they tend to be the concepts that make those who are concerned with the development lose sleep over them, pondering to subscribe or not to subscribe, to adopt and how to adopt. Therefore, it is important that we have a critical understanding of those concepts.

It should not be surprising that those concepts need critical examination. For instance, "democracy" has meant many things to many people. It could mean a political process, and could also mean a proclamation to emphasize such values as equality, justice, and majority rule. How would it be to have an Asian democracy with Asian values embedded, or within an Asian context in a particular historical juncture in Asia? Also, does respecting an individual person necessarily lead to Western individualism? Individual rights are part of human rights. Is it, as some have made it to be, the most important one of all the human rights? Freedom has different aspects. To be emancipated from a poverty of things crucial to human well-being is certainly more important than the freedom of choice. And is the freedom of political choice more important than the freedom of social choice? People are born with different circumstances and different functional abilities. Are inequalities cases of natural facts or personal attitudes of the more fortunate and the more privileged against those less fortunate and less privileged? This book is not in a position to deal with and try to answer all those questions, but it will try to show how important it is for people who are concerned with development to be aware of the delicate distinctions in the meanings of these important concepts. For instance, many see respecting an individual person as one of the important characteristics of modernity, with which I agree. But, as I shall discuss in Chapter 1, respect for the individual person in the traditional Chinese sense is quite different from the sense of Western individualism. So, I disagree with some who say individual freedom has to presuppose Western individualism. Again, many see democracy as being very important to a modern society, with which I also agree. But we need to see that the democratic process itself is only a skeleton to which many values have to be added, as indeed, Western democracy comes with many values embedded, some of which are applicable to Asian countries and some not. Likewise, market economy seems to be able to release people's energy in creating wealth. But should a society let loose that raw market force without constraints? Therefore, what values are added into those systems would make a big difference to a non-Western country as to whether a system will be successful or not in that country. In the end, most important of all is that a society needs to carry with it a set of values accepted by the people of a particular country as significant enough to produce a cohesiveness and an esprit de corps to give momentum in development. In other words, when emerging societies move ahead in their development, aside from grappling with many complicated practical problems and issues, they have to deal with the meanings of concepts that guide their development. There are systems and institutions like the market economy, the democratic process. What is important for leaders of a developing country is to have an understanding of the different subtle implications involved in those systems and institutions, and of the need to have values with cultural identity undergirding those systems and institutions they want to adopt. Without the understanding and awareness of the subtleties, the development would result in not having the clarity of direction nor the energy of the general population behind it. This misfortunate phenomenon has been borne out amply well by the earlier modern history of China.

In a nutshell, the methodology being suggested here is a two-prong approach with concept analysis and cultural identity working together as follows:

- Critical analysis of different aspects and meanings of concepts important to a contemporary modern society.
- Identify deep-seated and most cherished values in one's heritage. This is the sense of "cultural identity" used in this book.

- Use cultural identity as resources to evaluate and understand the important concepts, and also as criteria to evaluate historical outcomes of decisions made.
- Set priority and appropriate timing of implementing the programmes derived from those concepts;

The important point of the methodology is that, while a developing country needs an effective and efficient way to modernize, it should not lose sight of the awareness of one's heritage, a true perspective of one's own history and a unique cultural identity in this world much influenced by globalization. This identity is of utmost importance to a people's national psyche. For, it provides continuity and direction as well as a sense of dignity to the country, thereby giving confidence to it as a responsible member of the world community. And concept analysis is important because it prevents the development from going into useless or even harmful directions.

To emphasize cultural identity is not to say that the West has a definition of contemporary modernity and Asia has its own definition of contemporary modernity, but rather that we have taken concepts that have been prevalently considered by people in both the East and the West as nominally important for modernization. My suggestion is only that the exact understanding of the concepts, in order to be relevant to a particular culture, has to be evaluated by that country's cultural values. Since the fundamental criteria to judge and decide what is relevant and what is significant for a particular country depends on whether it will or will not awake the people's drive and creativity, cultural identity becomes central to this process.

While emphasizing the importance of cultural traditions of different countries, I should also clarify another significant point. With due deference to Samuel Huntington's most important book *The Clash of Civilizations and the Remaking of World Order*, I have seen different cultures co-existing without clashes; neither will my emphasis on cultural identity necessarily lead to clashes of cultures. Although that book somehow made prognostications of the 9/11 event in 2001, and the subsequent events in Afghanistan of 2002 and Iraq of 2003, the clash of civilizations is not a historical necessity in all instances and at all places. If we define civilization as an extension of culture as Huntington does, we see that there are places where people with many very different ethnic, religious, and cultural backgrounds living together peacefully. For example in Malaysia, Muslims, Christians, Hindus, Buddhists, and Confucians live together side-by-side generally without clashes, despite the affirmative action program that benefits the Malays, at least under the 22 years of governance by Mahathir Mohamad. There are 56 ethnic groups in China: the Han majority and 55 minority nationalities. As a whole, they live together peacefully, with their own languages, religions, and cultural traditions. This is not to say that there are no minor pockets of people inside and outside of China wanting to stir up racial antagonism. Of course, the peaceful co-existence of these ethnic, cultural, and religious groups is only possible with a certain philosophical outlook and carefully devised policies and laws.[18] Realizing the severe consequences of ethnic, cultural or religious frictions, the Chinese laws concerning nationalities are very strict on the behavior of the Han majority group. Often a civil offence in an ordinary situation, such as a man seducing a young woman, could turn out to be a criminal offence if she was from a minority nationality, unless he marries the woman. Further to laws, there are policies in China to preserve the cultures of various nationalities. Universities and institutions have been established specifically to study those minority cultures, including studying and initiating performances of songs and dances of various minority nationalities to strengthen their cultural identity as well as enriching the fabric of the Chinese culture as a whole. Another example is that the Tibetan Institute has recorded over 5000 tapes of the Tibetan epic poem *Ge-Sa-Er* (格萨尔), which is twice as long as Homer's *Iliad* and *Odyssey* plus the Babylonia and Indian epic poems all put together, to preserve the oral tradition of the Tibetan culture.[19]

---

[18] *A Collection of Chinese Laws and Regulations to Guarantee Urban Ethnic Minorities' Right and Interests*, pp. 165–209

[19] 降边嘉措 '中国的伟大史诗 (*The Great Epic Poem of China*) 在北大听讲座 (*Lectures at Beijing University*) Vol. 9, pp. 283–295.

It should be pointed out-here that only God could forgive a third party who, for political purpose and economic reasons, tries to subvert a country by stirring up religious or racial hatred. History has records of too many of such activities which invariably end up gruesomely bloody and tragic.

So, this book presupposes that it is possible for different countries, with their own cultural interpretations of sociopolitical concepts and cultural identity, to live together peacefully. After all, harmony does not necessarily imply homogeneity, and unity does not have to imply uniformity.

In working out a solution, I have said that we not only need to dissect the prevalent concepts, but also need to have an honest look at one's own culture. Using this principle to examine Chinese heritage, for example, this book's assertions are as follows:

A. The universal respect for law (law above everyone, including the law-maker) is a positive contribution of Western civilization which was never there in the Chinese tradition, but is crucial for a contemporary modern society.

B. The respect for the individual person was always there in the Chinese tradition, but not in the same sense as Western individualism.

C. The demand for freedom is a universal human demand, and not an invention of any one culture.

D. The concept of equality was always there in the Chinese tradition, as shown by the examination system through which anybody could change his socioeconomic and political status.

E. Human rights includes values, some of which China always had, but the idea about "rights" presuppose a guarantee by a universal respect of law that the China heritage did not have.

F. Democracy as a political process being practiced in the Western world today was never there in the Chinese tradition, but many values akin to those embraced by democracy were in the Chinese heritage.

Since the fundamental criteria for judging what is relevant and what is significant for a particular culture depend on the deep-seated and most cherished values of that culture, we shall find that those values are most likely embraced by an understanding of Man in that culture. Therefore, I shall start this study with the concept of personhood, for everything else will be impacted by that understanding and flow from its implications.

Having said the above, I should point out that it is not the purpose of this book to propose any model of development for Asian countries. First, I do not have the knowledge of various cultures and their possible interpretations of the concepts to suggest a model of development for all countries. Second, even if I had, I do not believe a single model would be applicable to all developing countries. Therefore, this being a book mainly on methodology, it will only cite specific cases of cultural identity as examples. The real work of identifying deep-seated and most cherished values of a culture is a prolonged process involving the dedication and debates of a great many people concerned in each particular country. Leaders in those countries, however, might use the method as a guide to rethink those important concepts and try to understand them in relation to their own cultural identity and development, and come up with their own solutions without either embracing wholeheartedly or rejecting totally those concepts at face value. Therefore, each chapter of the book is an example of the analysis of those prevalent concepts.

Lastly, I would like to state that this book is primarily for those readers who think that such concepts as individualism, capitalism, freedom, and democracy are the characteristics of contemporary modernity. We should adopt them wholeheartedly and that all traditional values are irrelevant to this age. It is also for those readers who, after seeing the tragedies of two world wars initiated by a Western power in the last century, the decadence that exist in Western societies and the arrogance and unilateralism of a Western power today that has trampled international laws, national sovereignty, and human dignity, want to reject everything Western and to revive their own traditions in totality, like Hinduism in India or

Confucianism in China. It is furthermore for those readers who, after seeing the collapse of Communist countries in Eastern Europe in the late 1980s and China's adoption of the market economy earlier, think those phenomena represent a de facto vindication of capitalism and Western democracy, and hence think that there is no longer any use for Marxism today. To all those readers, I would like to suggest that it is not enough to have, for instance, dialogues between western and traditional cultures, between Marxism and the market economy or between centralized democracy and western democracy. I urge them to see that the issues before us are much more complex, and also to urge them to remember that all mighty rivers are the confluence of many minor streams which are fed by trickles of water from the melting ice of high mountains. So are important ideas for development in a new age. Our world today is too dynamic to be understood and managed merely from the wisdom of any one or two cultural heritages.

Respect for the Individual Person and Individualism

A critical part of the methodology of understanding the appropriateness of a sociopolitical concept for a particular society is by analyzing it in that society's cultural and historical contexts. One of the most fundamental differences between Western and Asian understandings of important sociopolitical concepts stems from a different view of the concept of personhood. It will be obvious from this discussion that respect for the individual person, which is a basic tenet of contemporary modernity is not the same as individualism of the Western liberal tradition as in the traditional Chinese sense. This difference has significant implications in other prevalent concepts to be studied in this book, and also has implications in Western, especially American, foreign policies. It is essential, then, that we begin our discussion with the concept of personhood.

This difference between Western individualism and the traditional Chinese way of looking at the individual person has already been pointed out by many scholars, and conscious application of this understanding in practical governance was, for example, promoted by the former Prime Minister of Singapore, Lee Kuan Yew.

He advocated governing by the Confucian ideal, emphasizing, among other things, public well-being, collective welfare system, security of livelihood, development and economic prosperity. It became well known as the "Singapore School".[1] But due to the fact that Singapore is a city state, whose economy depends heavily on tourism, it cannot afford to have social turmoil. Thus, the government tends to give social order and security higher priority over individual rights, resulting in it being considered a strongly controlled state, whereas my reading of the Chinese tradition would give much more freedom to the individual person. Some writers, in differentiating the Western and the Chinese traditional view of personhood, tend to emphasize the positive value of community-oriented harmony in Confucianism. But a more comprehensive summary of the Chinese philosophy on personhood are as follows: Comprehensive harmonization, creative development, benevolence for humanity and community, self-reflection (and self-cultivation), freedom for the individual person, vision and faith in human life and human spirituality.[2] In other words, there has been a tendency to think of Confucian understanding of a person only in a social sense and to neglect its tremendous emphasis on respect for the individual person. Thus, I shall call attention to the independence of a person as well as his/her relation to the community or state in the Chinese tradition.

In order to make clearer the difference between the two concepts of personhood, I shall first trace the background of the Western tradition of individualism. The individual in Western political thinking is understood as the basic autonomous unit of a society. Stemming from the Judeo-Christian tradition, an individual is understood as unique before God: God talked to Abraham and Moses personally and believers talk to God directly in prayers. Man and God, as Martin Buber puts it, is in an "I and Thou" relationship[3] such that the individual becomes sacred and invulnerable, and

---

[1] See Robert Cassen, "Democracy and Development" in *Democracy, Human Rights and Economic Development*, p. 44.

[2] Editor's Note, *Journal of Chinese Philosophy*, September–December, 2003, p. 286.

[3] Martin Buber, *I and Thou*.

autonomous among his/her fellow human beings. Following this Judeo-Christian lineage, the whole liberal democratic tradition from Hobbes and Locke feeding into the Enlightenment tradition and John Stuart Mill[4] presupposed an autonomous individual juxtaposed against the state in their discussions of liberty and political rights. According to that tradition, a society is only a group of individuals bound together by their voluntary covenant to live together and commitment to observe certain rules for the sake of their social needs. It could be best represented by Jean J. Rousseau's book, *The Social Contract*. Of course, all the earlier thinkers emphasized the fact that individuals could not survive without a collective association, which was the sovereign state. But they took the state only as a necessary evil for individuals' self-preservation. The state could also be tyrannical and liable to abuse the power it had. Therefore, while condoning its necessity, they all wanted to extricate the individual from the power of the state to recapture the individual's "native liberty".[5] To Rousseau, the voluntary subjugation of the individual was to the "general will" that represented the common good of a society, instead of to a sovereign state.[6] Nevertheless, he still saw the ideal for an individual was a return to the uncorrupted natural existence of a "natural savage".[7] This individualism became further developed in the New World of America as exemplified by the writings of Ralph Waldo Emerson[8] and Henry David Thoreau.[9] Self-reliant individualism was developed to its fullest in America, and permeated all political ideas and social values in American thinking. Even John Dewey, who attempted to speak to the age of industrialization and individual empiricism and talked about "social planning", was individualistic

---

[4] See Thomas Hobbes, *Leviathan*, especially pp. 128–152.
   John Locke, *Two Treatises of Government*, especially pp. 93–98.
   John Stuart Mill, *Utilitarianism and On Liberty*, especially pp. 131–146.
[5] David Hume, *Political Essays*, pp. 187–188.
[6] Jean J. Rousseau, *The Social Contract and Other Later Political Writings*, especially pp. 39–81.
[7] Jean J. Rousseau, *Discourses on Origin of Inequality of Men* pp. 88–89.
[8] George Kateb, *Emerson and Self Reliance*, pp. 1–ff.
[9] Henry David Thoreau, *Walden and Civil Disobedience*, pp. 224–243.

at the base of his philosophy. As Ralph Ketcham observes: "Though Dewey later explained this process in works like *The Public and Its Problems* (1927) and *A Common Faith* (1934) using terms similar to those used by the late twentieth century communitarians, he understood it as in new liberalism retaining the emphasis on individual enhancement of the 'old liberals', Locke, Adam Smith and Mill....."[10] Nowadays, the communitarian, Marxist and non-liberal feminist philosophers in America are beginning to remind people of the unique importance of the community. They observe that there is "an excessive individualism in the liberal democratic tradition" in the way that it places "too much attachment on the self as an autonomous chooser", and not enough emphasis on the individual's "social role in assessing its social arrangement".[11] Despite these recent philosophers' cautions, however, individualism is still the basis of American mainstream thinking today. This individualism in America, actualized to its extreme form in personal life, is the absolute unconditional demand for free speech and free expression, even to the extent of justifying the publishing of pornography; in family life, it is the priority given to personal achievement and success over concern and care for one's parents and senior citizens; in community life, it is exemplified by the insistence on the individual's right to own weapons, despite many incidents of tragic killings of innocent schoolchildren by irresponsible gun owners;[12] in political life, it is actualized in the top priority given to the exercising of individual rights in free elections. This last insistence is understandably important to Americans. I do not query the legitimacy of that priority for Americans, but when that priority gets translated into foreign policy, it means that America has been promoting American-style democracy worldwide as the number one priority,

---

[10] Ralph Ketcham, *The Idea of Democracy in Modern Era*, p. 83.

[11] Robert Simon, "Introduction" in *Blackwell's Guide to Social and Political Philosophy*, pp. 8–11.

[12] For instance: on April 20, 1999 at Columbine High School, Littleton, Colorado; on March 25, 1998 at Jonesboro High School, Jonesboro, Arkansas; and on May 21, 1998 at Thurston High School, Springfield, Oregon.

even though the conditions might not be ripe in a particular developing country.

We have just seen that, for instance, according to the Chinese view, an individual is inextricable from his/her community. Individuals do not deliberately form a society, but are born into families situated in a society. In fact, an individual person is defined by his/her membership of a community, or in sociological terms, by his/her social roles. One achieves personhood by being a son/daughter, brother/sister, father/mother, uncle/aunt, or a citizen of one's motherland etc. These roles are not by choice but by birth.

In the Chinese tradition (often in this book I am using Confucianism as a developed tradition and not necessarily the original teachings of Confucius himself), the most central concept in Confucianism is *ren* (仁 has been translated as "respectful", "forgiving", "trustworthy", "sensitive" or "benevolent"). It is all about one's relationship with others.[13] As Robert Neville, quoting Tu Weiming, put it, *ren* implies "human-relatedness".[14] Lee Yearley also concluded: "The commitment to the community on the part of the Chinese goes with an understanding that the support of the total community and even of the entire natural world is necessary to sustain the full development and expression of the individual."[15]

Confucianism, however, while confirming the social nature of a person, stresses at the same time the importance of the individual person. A person is much respected for his potential and much is expected of his character and responsibility. For instance, the virtue of a noble person can be described by the notion: "One can capture the highest general of an army, but no one can subdue a person's will (or character)".[16] For the intellectual members of the society, their responsibility is even heavier. As the Song Dynasty writer, Fan Zhongyan, following the Confucian tradition, wrote: "Before the rest

---

[13] Feng Yulan (冯友兰), *A Short History of Chinese Philosophy* (中国哲学简史), pp. 37.

[14] Robert Neville, *Boston Confucianism*, pp. 97–99.

[15] "Virtue and Religious Virtue in the Confucian Tradition" in *Confucian Spirituality*, p. 54.

[16] 三军可夺帅也，匹夫不可夺志也.

of the world worries, I worry, and only after the rest of the world is happy, can I then be happy."[17] Also, in the standard format of 2000 years of continuous historical records, there is one category specifically dedicated to biographies of important personalities. Such is the Confucian tradition of respecting the individual person. One has dignity, compassion and social conscience[18] that deserve respect and is honored for one's ability to self-cultivate and gain moral stature, but at the same time, one is never completely autonomous and metaphysically independent from the community and nature one is in.[19]

Another tradition that is just as important as Confucianism in the Chinese heritage is Daoism.[20] Both these traditions viewed the individual person as a part of nature; namely a holistic view of man and nature (天人合一). Thomas Berry, writing about the Chinese person, puts it: "No human mode of existence, of activity, or of value is possible except in a natural or social context... To awaken our individual to a consciousness of one's individual personality in this context is the obligation of the society. The importance of this consciousness and this discipline can be seen when we consider how the entire order of universe rests on the individual."[21] To grasp this view further, we have to

---

[17] 先天下之忧而忧，后天下之乐而乐.

[18] The Chinese have been considered insensitive to public order, such as spitting and littering in public. But those are habits from ignorance of public health knowledge just as the industrialized countries were once ignorant of the hazards of industrial smoke and chemical waste. But that insensitivity to public order is quite different from the value of social consciousness of larger community welfare that we are talking about.

[19] I cannot understand how Tamney and Chiang could consider Confucius "did not teach about the dignity of the person as such". Perhaps the following lines explain it when they said: "... it [Confucius' teaching] can be seen as perhaps an underdeveloped counterpart to the notion of individualism". In other words, they are using Western individualism to judge Confucius' teaching. They also claimed Western individualism as one of the important elements of modernity, and to that view, of course, this book takes strong exception (Tammey and Chiang, pp. 38–58).

[20] Daoist thought was also important for its influence on Buddhism when it came to China from India to form a Chinese version of Buddhism that had great influence on Chinese culture. (Chan Buddhism is known as Zen Buddhism in Japan).

[21] "Individualism and Holism in Chinese Tradition: The religious context", in *Confucian Spirituality*, p. 49.

understand it from the point of view of what Sir Arthur Eddington calls the "continuum logic", which does not separate completely the subject and the object of knowing — the observer and that being observed — as we have learned from the modern study of highly complex biological process.[22] In this sense, a person derives his values and character from nature's Way, and nature also supports the person in what he is and what he does according to nature's Way.[23] Nature has both its harmonious aspect like the ant and bee "societies", together with the ecological balance of the elements; and also its individual creative and spontaneous aspect like the soaring and sprinting of birds and beasts, the growing and thrusting of flowers and trees or the flowing and surging of rivers and ocean waves. While the Confucian tradition, alluding to the cosmic origin of the virtues of harmony, emphasizes a person's responsibility to a social nexus, Daoism, alluding to the cosmic origin of the creative spirit, stresses the spontaneity and free-spirited nature of the individual person.[24] Thus, in Confucianism, while a person is honored, respected and is expected to have moral cultivation, one is not autonomous but inextricably bound to the community one is in. Conversely, with Daoism, while the community is important, respect for a person's freedom, creativity and spontaneity is crucial. For, within the community, the individual person continually "seeks to increase human freedom and to act creatively, spontaneously and flexibly; such freedom is achieved by molding oneself on the Tao itself".[25] This freedom and spontaneity, when related to political life, is characterized by the notion of *wu wei* (无为) which has often been translated before as "non-action". But now the general consensus of scholars is that it should be understood as "non-coercive

---

[22] See Walter Benesch and Edmond Wilner, "Continuum Logic: A Chinese Contribution to Knowledge and Understanding in Philosophy and Science" *Journal of Chinese Philosophy*, pp. 472–474.

[23] See Tang Junyi (唐君毅), *The Spiritual Value of Chinese Culture or The Value of the Chinese Cultural Spirit* (both meanings are in the book) (中国文化之精神价值), pp. 134–138.

[24] See *Ibid*, pp. 204–205.

[25] Jess Fleming, "Self and (in)finitude: Embodiment and the Other" *Journal of Chinese Philosophy*, p. 177.

action"; meaning that if a ruler follows the cosmic Way, he should not do anything forcibly. That is why, although there had been Daoists in officialdom historically, the general tendency for Daoists was to keep their hands off the legal and bureaucratic strictures of the political reality.[26] So, the Chinese tradition has a dual-centered understanding of the individual person, and these dual aspects are united.

To take an example from real life, we see at a critical moment and at the most essential level, the private person and his public consideration are inseparable. In 2005 the China Central Television Network selected a young man named Wei Qinggang (魏青刚) as one of several young people to have impacted the society in very important ways that year. The young man came from a rural area to work in a big city as a construction worker. One day, as he passed by the seashore during stormy weather, seeing a girl engulfed in the waves of over 2 meters high (as shown in the video footage), he jumped into the ocean, without hesitation, to save the girl not once but three times because the big waves separated them the first two times, and he had to come ashore to recuperate. This incident reminds us of the example used by Mencius[27] to indicate a person's innate capacity for compassion toward another human being, that one would naturally help a boy in danger of falling into a well. I shall allude to that example later, but the example of Wei Qinggang tells us that, at a critical moment, there is no distance between the "will of the self" and the "action for others", though the young man was certainly a free individual, taking action of his own free will, and was accountable for the consequence to himself as well as to others. And he certainly did not feel he did it out of moral consideration, or to be recognized as a public-spirited hero, as indicated by the fact that he was very low-key about the incident, according to his co-workers at the construction site. The public only knew about the extraordinary incident 3 days later from an onlooker's video footage. We can be sure that this young man, with his background, would not

---

[26] See Russell Kirkland, *Taoism — The Enduring Tradition*, p. 26, and Roger Ames and David Hall, *Daodejing*, p. 38.

[27] Mencius, a well-known later disciple and proponent of earlier Confucianism.

have read the Confucian classic by Mencius. Nevertheless, he displayed that traditional Chinese concept of personhood: a person can be both a free-spirited individual person and, at the same time, naturally inclined to feel that he is part of a community larger than he himself. Granted, we found out later that he had saved two little girls before in the river of his native village. But that fact only tells us his confidence in his own swimming ability, and does not diminish the nobility of his natural inclination to dive into the high waves. Nor does it minimize his courage in tackling ocean waves over 2 meters high, when he is only used to the water condition of a river.

In less critical situations, for example, a traditional Chinese official's public activity might require more reflection and less dramatic action, and yet both his reflection as a private person and his sense of social responsibility toward public affairs show that they are integral parts of his personality. Listen to the Tang Dynasty official and poet *Du Fu* (杜甫, 712–770) about how he would still want to be useful to society, even though he was ill and out of favor in officialdom, just as a jaded horse should be kept for its experience in knowing the path, though it could no longer go long distances.

ON RIVER HAN

by Du Fu

On River Han my home thoughts fly,
Bookworm with worldly ways in fright.
The cloud and I share the vast sky;
I'm lonely as the moon all night.
My heart won't sink with the sinking sun;
Autumn wind blows illness away.
A jaded horse kept for [what's done],
Though it cannot go a [distant] way.[28]

[Author's rendition]

---

[28] *Bilingual Edition 300 Tang Poems*, p. 295.

The private individual's inextricability from public affairs is no–where better portrayed than by the well-known Confucian ideal quoted above: "Before the world worries, I worry, and only after the world is happy can I then be happy".

One may ask how it is possible to hold a view that says an individual is inseparable from a community together with a view that he is a free-spirited individual person. It is incomprehensible because we are bound by our "either/or" form of thought, which, according to Sir Arthur Eddington, is a primitive form of thought.[29] In practical life, aside from the continuum logic, we often use "both/and" logic like the moral demand for both love and justice, both forgiveness and judgment in the Christian tradition; and the demand for both majority rule and civil disobedience, both liberty and equality in Western political thought. In Buddhism, there is also "neither/nor" logic, such as the second stage of Buddhist philosophy which proclaims that reality consists of neither real elements nor unreal elements; and in the universe, things neither originate nor disappear.[30]

Some may have difficulty in accepting the both/and kind of logic, because they tend to view things statically. For that, I would like to say a few more words. First of all, we are not dealing with "definition" for which either/or logic is most appropriate. When we are dealing with a person and his/her community, we are dealing with a relationship in human activity which I propose is not static but a process. For that, the both/and logic is most appropriate. Hegel's dialectic logic also emphasizes the process of understanding phenomena, but it is more appropriate for explaining the relationships of large historical events. For what we encounter in everyday life, I think the both/and logic is more appropriate, though they are similar in that both stress the process in logical understanding of phenomena. Perhaps the both/and process logic is more attuned to the Asian way of thinking. As the great process philosopher, Alfred North Whitehead, wrote in *Process and Reality*, the general position

---

[29] See Footnote 22.
[30] Stcherbatsky, *Buddhist Logic*, Vol. I, pp. 8–9.

of his philosophy of organism "seems to approximate more to some strains of Indian or Chinese thought than to Western Asiatic or European thought. One side makes process ultimate; the other side makes fact ultimate".[31]

A good example of both/and logic used in our public lives can be taken from one of Mao Zedong's famous demands, asking the production of the country to be "more", "fast", "good" and "economical".[32] People used to chuckle under their breath about such silly demands, thinking it is impossible to produce good-quality products if they had to make them quickly in large quantities and in a cost-saving way. That is quite true in a relatively static working environment, say, of a hand craftsman's situation. If he had to produce carvings of jade figures in large quantities very quickly and save on material and labor, it would indeed be impossible to produce good-quality products. But now consider manufacturing as an extended complicated process: those demands become quite possible. In fact, the very reason how Dell is able to be competitive is precisely because it is able to produce good functional and reliable computers in large quantity and quickly through a made-to-order system whereby your order can be delivered to your doorstep the next day (in America). At the same time, production costs are cut through: rational design of the product in order to save labor in assembly; economy of scale in ordering parts; a just-in-time system of delivery of parts to save warehousing and inventory cost; and fast capital turn-around to save the cost of money. When manufacturing is considered in such a process, we see that seemingly contradictory demands in the either/or logical environment become not so contradictory, but reasonable in the both/and logical environment.

Likewise, concerning the relationship between the individual person and the community or state, it is also never static but always in a process. In the first place, the object of loyalty is not a static

---

[31] As quoted by Yih-Hsien Yu in "Two Chinese Philosophers and Whitehead Encountered" *Journal of Chinese Philosophy*, September, 2005, p. 239.

[32] "多, 快, 好, 省". I am not sure whether Mao was conscious of using both/and logic when he made that demand, though he often spoke dialectically.

entity. When we say a person should be loyal to the state, it is not loyalty to an entity, but to a process that we call history of a country. That person is certainly not asked to be loyalty to a particular administration of a government. One is rather asked to be loyal to the country's history, in all its richness of glories and sorrows, as well as its commitment to high ideals and its unfortunate failures; the whole history which one is proud to be a member of. Secondly, while the object of loyalty is a process, so is the relationship of the person to it. One grows to identify with that history via a process. Once identified with that history, it does not matter so much where one lives and what one's tastes are, or what kind of traveling document one holds. It has even less to do with how one dresses, what kind of music, art or food one prefers, One is not considered Americanized just because one frequents McDonalds or likes jazz or rock music, any more than one is considered Sinicized just because one frequents Chinese restaurants and appreciates Chinese art. Thus, loyalty to one's country lies in one's identification with the history of that country; whether one rejoices or whether one is indifferent at the successful moments of that country, or whether one weeps inside or whether one laughs and ridicules at its failing moments. By the same token, when this book criticizes the foreign policies of a particular administration of a country, it is not to criticize the whole history of that country that has been created by generations of courageous people; neither is it to criticize the people who have been nurtured by the full richness of that history.

Similarly, in being obedient to the laws of the state, the relationship is also not static but in a process. For laws are always stated on certain conditions, and the citizens should always behave in certain circumstances. So, we cannot ask blankly which is more important: an individual's rights or the state's prerogatives? For the answer is always: "It all depends". This is not relativism, because the values and principles behind the laws are not relative, but plainly stated. It is rather that the application of the laws is subject to circumstances. For example, there can be very specific laws like: "It is a crime to kill another person", or "It is a crime to steal things". The answer is still "It all depends" on the circumstances of the killing and stealing.

The relationship between the individual and the state is a complex process just as manufacturing is a complex process. The variables can sometimes be settled only through a process. So, an individual may be both obedient to the law and disobedient, depending on whether a particular requirement of the state is or is not reasonable according to the individual's basic rights, and whether a particular action by the individual is or is not contrary to the reasonable obligation of citizens to the state.

A personal experience might illuminate the point. When I was a student in America, I was quite active in the Chinese Students' Association. I guess that fact alone caught the notice of the FBI during the McCarthy era in America.[33] Then, as president of the association, I made a few mistakes, like unintentionally rescheduling a dancing party to fall on October 1st, which happened to be the national day of the People's Republic of China, an enemy of America during the Cold-War days. And again, unknowingly, I staged, on approximately the same days as Beijing was staging an English translation of a Chinese play, *Thunderstorm*, which is about complicated personal relationships in a feudal family meeting the challenges of modernity, and in which a worker, in one line, called the head of the family a capitalist. I was interviewed by the FBI several times about the intention of these incidents. In the ultimate one, I was asked that famous question: "If there was a war between the United States and Communist China, which side would you be on?". Although I got off the hook by answering that, on religious grounds, I was against wars in general, the question still lingered in my mind for a long time. Aside from the fact that their suspicion of me was unfounded, and charges of many others on the ground of "guilt by association" was legally unjustifiable, I now see that people's

---

[33] After WWII, America was afraid that some wanted to turn the country toward Socialism, and thus there was a movement of "witch-hunting" for Communists and Communist sympathizers, among whom many innocent people, including Hollywood actors and actresses, were implicated. And during the 1950s, Senator Joseph McCarthy was a staunch advocate of that movement; hence the era was called "the McCarthy era".

See David H. Fischer, *Liberty and Freedom*, pp. 589–593 (for McCarthyism).

unconditional allegiance is not supposed to be toward an entity or a governmental administration. As citizens, people should hold allegiance to the deep-seated and most cherished values that have made up the country's history and culture with all their richness and imperfections, together with all the glories and sorrows that they have identified. In this sense, we can understand how a person can be both loyal and disobedient to the administration of a government. Likewise, the state has meaningful sovereignty over the citizens only if its laws and policies are based upon the deep-seated and most cherished values in the country's heritage.

That the both/and relationship between citizens and the laws of the state is a process can be further illuminated by the fact that, even after years of experience, large accumulation of legal cases and very specific laws on the respective rights and obligations of the citizens and the state, there is still a need for law courts to adjudicate extraordinary cases. The whole relationship between the state and its citizens is that of a complex process. That is why, concerning a person's legal rights and obligations, the due process of law is so important, for the true circumstances of the case may only be clarified through a process of investigation, challenging/defending and adjudication.

Without getting too involved in a discussion of logic, it suffices to say here that both/and logic operates in many facets of our lives. Thus, it is not unreasonable to have a concept of personhood that can be socially and individually considered. Ernst Cassia considered that man, growing out of an animal nature, is all at once a "political man", a "social man", an "economic man" and a "cultural man".[34] Among those descriptions, the first three are social in nature, and the last one is free, private, reflective, spontaneous and individual in nature. In practical life, individuals cannot survive without the environment provided by the community for social order, economic exchanges and ideational communication. Even Descartes, the foundation of whose philosophy was the autonomous individual, in his letter to Elizabeth Bohemia in 1645, had to confess that "none of us

---

[34] Hong Leili, "On Human Nature and Development in the Dao of Human Administration" in *Journal of Chinese Philosophy*, June 2003, p. 253.

could survive alone... the interest of the whole, of which he is a part, must always be preferred to those of our own particular person". But it was not clear when Descartes would put community first, and when the individual first.[35] It is, however, clear that according to traditional Chinese understanding as discussed above, both are important, and if there is a conflict of interest, precedence would go to the community when the rights of the individual are specified, because the community has the responsibility to do the greatest good to the greatest number of people (Utilitarianism). I shall deal with the issue of the protection of minority interests in another place. It can be stressed here initially that minority interests can be taken care of by legislation based on values protecting minority rights; like legal protection of the disabled, the marginalized sector of society (migrant workers in the city), the minority nationalities and so on in China today. Therefore, when there is a conflict of interests between the public life the individual person, and providing the rights of the individual are precisely specified, social concerns and human rights would take precedence over individual rights, social welfare over individual welfare, and social stability over individual whims. In private life, a person would exercise his free-spirited spontaneity, such as in religious worship, artistic expression, intellectual pursuits and scientific exploration. But one would need to be a "consequentialist" when relating to public affairs. That is what we mean by "responsible citizenship", "responsible social critique" and "responsible journalism" etc. Such is the relationship between a person's private life and public life in the traditional Chinese sense: One is a self-respecting and honourable person making free decisions, but is always mindful that one is what one is because one has been nurtured by one's family, given the benefits, encouragements and opportunities by one's immediate community, or even the international community, and nourished by nature's endowments. Therefore, one has responsibility toward the intimate, immediate and larger communities one lives in, and

---

[35] Cecilia Wee, "Descartes and Mencius on Self and Community", *Journal of Chinese Philosophy*, June, 2002, p. 194.

toward nature whose air, water and the refreshment of the general environment have sustained one with health and sanity.

A note of clarification is necessary. Responsibility toward the larger community indicated here is not the same as unconditional allegiance, as has already been alluded to in the example of being both loyal and disobedient in one's political context. The position taken here is not like that of Socrates, when he declined the opportunity to escape from prison but obeyed the Athenian court's decision on punishment and drank the poisonous hemlock, even though he knew he was right. His argument was that, having been nurtured and educated by the Athenian state of which he was a citizen, he had to obey the law of the state, right or wrong.[36] But that is not the position according to the traditional Chinese concept of personhood. Historically, there have been plenty of examples of Chinese officials making positive recommendations to change existing laws,[37] or retreating to live as a recluse in defiance against an unjust system. In either case, from the poems they wrote, we do not see an unconditional allegiance, but rather, a tremendous sense of responsibility toward the larger community they were in. For example, in the poem, *Song of the Conscripts*, Du Fu bemoaned the miseries of the people caused by conscription to fight the emperor's senseless wars. And Wang Anshi (王安石 1021–1086), one-time prime minister of the Northern Song Dynasty, lamented the extravagance and decadence in court lives in his poem, *Fragrance of Laurel Branches*.

SONG OF THE CONSCRIPTS

by Du Fu

Chariots rumble
And horses grumble.
The conscripts march with bows and arrows at the waist.

---

[36] See Plato's *Crito*.

[37] The reforms of Fan Zhongyan (范仲淹), Ouyang Xiu (欧陽修) and Wang Anshi (王安石), to name only a few. See Roberts, *A History of China*, pp. 89–92.

Their fathers, mothers, wives and children come in haste
To see them off; the bridge is shrouded with dust they've raised.
They clutch at their coats, stamp the feet and bar the way;
Their grief cries loud and strikes the cloud straight, straightaway.
An onlooker by the roadside ask an enrollee.
"The conscript is frequent", says he.
Some went north at fifteen to guard the rivershore,
And were sent west to till the land at forty-four.
The elder bound their young heads when they went away;
Just home, they're sent to the frontier though their hair's grey.
The field on borderland becomes a sea of blood;
The emperor's greed for land is still at high flood.
Have you not heard.
Two hundred districts east of the Hua Mountains lie,
Where briers and brambles grow in villages far and nigh.[38]

FRAGRANCE OF LAUREL BRANCHES

by Wang Anshi

I climb the height
And stretch my sight:
Late Autumn just begins its gloomy time.
The ancient capital looks sublime.
The limpid river, beltlike, flows a thousand miles;
Emerald peaks on peaks tower in piles.
In the declining sun sails come and go;
Against west wind wineshop streamers flutter high and low.
The painted boat
In cloud afloat,
Like stars in Silver River egrets fly.
What a picture before the eye!
The days gone by
Saw people in opulence vie.

---

[38] *Billingual Edition 300 Tang Poems* (兵车行), pp. 231, 233. This is only half of a long
poem, but it is enough to express the sentiments discussed in the text of this book.

Alas! Shame on shame came under the walls,
In palace halls.
Leaning on rails, in vain I utter sighs
Over ancient kingdoms' fall and rise.
The running water saw the Six Dynasties pass,
But I see only chilly mist and withered grass.
Even now and again
The songstress still sings
The song composed in vain
By a captive king.[39]

So, in the traditional Chinese sense, the individual, as a free-spirited moral person, has principles and character, and will rise to criticize the wider community when necessary, but at the same time, he/she is always conscious of his/her bond with, and indebtedness to, that community.

John Stuart Mill once wrote: "The worth of the State, in the long run, is the worth of the individuals comprising it."[40] Practically speaking, the Chinese view would turn the statement around and say: The plight of the individuals, in the long run, is the worth of the state encompassing them. The situation of the overseas Chinese certainly vindicates this latter statement historically. When China was weak and poor, they had their heads bent low, and only after China has progressed, could their heads be held up high.

Before ending this chapter, let us examine two issues that are important to Western individualism: namely, individual liberty and rights of an individual. It is true that liberty, which the Western liberal democratic tradition stresses so much, was not mentioned at all in the Chinese tradition. It has been said that Confucianism stresses a great deal on personal responsibility, but not much on personal liberty. There are two reasons for it.

First, the words "liberty" and "freedom" stem from the same root. The former is used more in political connections, to mean freedom from arbitrary and despotic tyranny and the preservation of legal

---

[39] *Bilingual Edition 300 Song Lyrics* (桂枝香), pp. 115–117.
[40] John Stuart Mill, *Utilitarianism and On Liberty*, pp. 180.

rights, and less in connection with other kinds of freedom. Thus, when people say that Chinese tradition makes little mention of liberty, it could mean only that the Confucian tradition had little to say about political freedom, and not freedom in other spheres. Second, it is a consensus of most scholars today that the ideal of equality is seminal to Confucianism. Confucius treated people equally, irrespective of their heredity or wealth, and perhaps only respective of their moral stature.[41] In fact, he said that in a country or a family, "one is not to worry about a lack of wealth, but only that the wealth is not equally distributed. A country is not to worry about too few people, but only about the lack of harmony among the people".[42] This concept of equality was the basis of his belief that ordinary people could be part of the government to advise the emperor on the running of the country. Thus, following this ideal, there were learning centers preparing ordinary citizens to take the examination for official posts in the early period of the Han Dynasty (206 BC–220 AD). Then, later, stretching till the late Qing Dynasty (1644–1911) for a total of about 2000 years, with brief interruptions in the Ming and Qing periods, China had an examination system to select government officials. And up to the end of the Song Dynasty (906 AD–1129 AD) after which the post of prime-ministership was eliminated, the examination system was even used to select prime ministers to head the affairs of the entire government (separate from the affairs of the royal family).[43] In other

---

[41] H.G. Creel, *Confucius and the Chinese Way*, p. 137 (See pp. 254–278 for discussion of Confucianism and Western thought).

[42] See *The Analects*, translated by Ezra Pound, p. 108. See also *Lun Yu Xin Jie* (论语新解), Vol. I by Qian Mu (钱穆), pp. 564–566.

According to Qian Mu, although the original text was "不患寡而患不均，不患贫而患不安", to understand the real meaning, it should read "不患贫而患不均，不患寡而患不安", because the phrases following the original text read "均无贫，和无寡，安无倾", meaning when there is equality, the lack of wealth would not be a matter of concern; when there is harmony, too few people would not be a matter of concern of the ruler.

[43] Qien Mu, *A Historical Overview of the Merits and Demerits of Chinese Political Structures* (中国历代政治得失), pp. 13–17. After the Song dynasty, in order to control the Han people during the foreign dynasties of Yuan and Qing, they abolished the system of having prime ministers in the government, and the Ming Dynasty did not restore it.

words, the Chinese tradition itself allowed ordinary citizens to participate and occupy even the highest position in the government. It was not necessary to fight on behalf of ordinary citizens against tyranny of the government as such. Of course, in practice there is always a gap between ideals and real practice. Historically, some emperors in China were stronger and more despotic. They overruled the prime ministers; while some prime ministers were strong enough to hold their forts and convinced the emperors that it was more prudent in maintaining their mandates to rule by following the Confucian ideals rather than being ruthless and oppressive. The point is, however, because of the existence of the ideal of equality and a selection system (albeit the content of the examination was imperfect in modern eyes) through which ordinary citizens could rise in social positions and participate in the affairs of governing and even head the whole governing process, explains why there was little assertion of political liberty in the Chinese tradition.

Secondly, the philosophy of Daoism itself stresses personal freedom, but it is freedom of a non-political nature. The Confucian ideal of government was to be concerned with the welfare of the populace, and promote satisfactory conditions for their livelihood.[44] The emperors, with the exception of taxation and military conscription, left the lives of their citizens and their economic activities pretty much alone. Therefore, there had not been a political necessity for a free-spirited individual in the Daoist sense to stand in opposition to the state. The dual-centered understanding of the individual person in the Chinese tradition was somewhat made possible by stressing Confucianism in one's public life and Daoism in one's private life. Historically, it was not unusual for an official to talk about Confucian ideals in office and Daoist thoughts of spontaneity out of the office.[45] One scholar observed that the reason why China was able to maintain peace and prosperity for hundreds of years, once upon a time, was its advocacy of a centralized government and, at

---

[44] See *Meng–Tzu*, translated by David Hinton, pp. 8–9.

[45] Ren Jiyu, "Why has the Influence of Confucianism and Daoist Thoughts Been so Profound and so Long-Lasting in China" in *Contemporary Chinese Thought* M.E. Sharpe (ed.) Fall, 1998, p. 42.

the same time, a self-sufficient economy that the government did not interfere with too much.[46] This dual nature of Chinese society was also observed by John K. Fairbank, who, in analyzing ancient Chinese society, noticed that while the government structure, being Confucian in its foundation, was static from the Ming to the Qing Dynasty, the economy was lively with free trade and had tremendous growth.[47] To the Daoists, liberty was not an issue, because they had a political philosophy of non-coercive action, and a tendency to keep their hands off politics; they were able to be free and spontaneous in their private lives. Therefore, according to what was discussed above about both/and logic, that dual-centeredness would not make a person schizophrenic.

It is also true that the Chinese tradition had little to say on individual rights. In Chapter 6, I shall indicate that the emphasis on legal rights and legal protection of a person is a very important positive contribution of Western civilization. It will be dealt with later so I shall not go into it here. What is relevant here is that the emphasis on legal rights lies not so much in the rights of the autonomous individual, as in stressing a person's entitlements needing legal guarantee and protection, rather than relying on the mercy of those in power. To specify an individual's entitled rights is important; what is even more important in practical political life is that those entitlements have legal protection. A Platonic philosopher-king or a Confucian benevolent emperor is always a historical possibility. For instance, there have indeed been wise and benevolent emperors in Chinese history. The point in political philosophy is that we cannot afford to depend on a benevolent and just ruler all the time, because sometimes a completely moral person could become corrupt after he has obtained power. As Lord Acton's famous saying goes: "Power tends to corrupt, and absolute power corrupts absolutely". Human beings are frail before all sorts of temptations, including the temptation of power. So, the citizens' entitlements have to be guaranteed legally by the universal rule of law. For our

---

[46] *Ibid*, p. 41.

[47] John K. Fairbank, *The Chinese: Adapting the Past, Facing the Future* Robert Deruberger *et al.* (eds.), p. 49.

discussion of individual rights here, the important point is not so much of the individual as the necessity of a legal system to protect the individual's rights.

This goes to say that just because there are rights belonging to individuals, it does not mean that they are necessarily evolved from the concept of individualism. We shall deal more with this issue in the next chapter. It should be mentioned here that those rights, in essence, belong to the whole of humanity. They are rights of an individual person, because that person is a member of humanity. For instance, to the Romans, legal rights to private property only belonged to Roman citizens and not to slaves or conquered people.[48] If they had considered the latter group of people also part of humanity, they would have no problem also giving them the rights on private property.

One may also ask, if respect for the individual is there in Chinese tradition, why was women's role so degrading and a great many of their lives so tragic? The answer, similarly, is that the plight of traditional Chinese women was not due to a lack of respect for the individual, but rather that women were not treated equally as men. Otherwise, it would be difficult to understand why there are still women's liberation movements in Western societies where respect for the individual has such a long tradition. To clarify this issue further, we should see that "institutions" are different from "cultural values".[49] The latter are accepted by people in a society for a very long time with theoretical basis, whereas the former could be forced upon people without consideration of values honored by the people in the society. It is like the shaving of hair and growing of pigtails that were forced upon the Han people in Qing Dynasty China by the Manchus. That institution was much opposed by the Han people, hence the existence of an edict by the Manchu government saying: "If you want to keep your head, you shave your hair; if

---

[48] Charles Montesquieu, *The Spirit of the Laws*, pp. 54–ff.

[49] This differentiation is indebted to Hia Xueluan, "The Origin, Development and Characteristics of Humanism in China" in *Lectures at Beijing University*, Vol. 5 pp. 105–122.

you want to keep your hair, you lose your head".[50] Institutions often have double standards of values for different people. The traditional roles of wives, concubines and widows in China were good examples of that, even though historically there were very strong women empresses and there were archival documents to indicate that divorces were allowed in the Tang Dynasty to free the women from unsuitable marriages. When the value of respecting all persons equally was instituted after 1949 in China, the situation for women changed very quickly. Although the society was, then, still divided into different strata, it was divided on the basis of "political reliability" and not on the basis of gender. Of course, in every society there is always a big difference between ideal and practical situations. Tradition dies hard. For instance, even today, many women in the rural areas still live according to their traditional subservient role. It is similar in the cities, even though they know they have been emancipated and have worked outside of their homes. I personally have had dinners with Chinese families, where the wives came from very traditional rural areas. There, the wives came to greet us, but always ate in the kitchen and never with us at the same table. This does not mean that the concept of equality is not generally accepted in the society. Nevertheless, because the Women's Liberation Movement, as far as it has touched the areas, was encouraged in China from top-down, calling attention to a basic, accepted value, women in China have not found it necessary to fight bitterly for their rights and pretend to be masculine. Consequently, there is now not the kind of animosity between women and men in China as in the West, especially in America before the 1960s; they could thereby retain their femininity while being independent and confident in various important political, social and economic roles. This is to say when an institution (not habits) can be demolished easily, the undergirding value is most likely not a deep-seated one. In the same token, when a new institution could be established quickly, it means that there are probably deep-seated values undergirding the new institution. What I am saying is that the concept of equality has

---

[50] "留头不留发，留发不留头" *Ibid*. pp. 105–122.

been there in the Chinese heritage. Of course, in practice, how far that concept has been carried out across the gender, ethnic, racial or cultural lines, is another question with which I shall deal in Chapter 4.

May I add here that in discussing the issue of gender equality and the likes of social issues, we have a tendency to skip from a discussion of ideals to that of the practical situation indiscriminately and end up confusing ourselves. It is a methodological mistake which I call "the fallacy of skipping the divide". Due to the inevitable divide between ideals and reality, we can often create a confused picture by comparing the ideals of one society with the practical situations of another society, or vice versa, making the comparison very unfair. For example, if I wanted to talk about America negatively, I can say: "Even though America has high-sounding ideals such as justice, equality and freedom, we see that there are much deplorable situations in reality about racial discrimination, the slum areas, the homeless people and the white supremacy societies like the Ku Klux Klan (more recently called the Imperial Klan of America) in the American society. In comparison, while another society's social situation might be backward, it at least has very high social ideals to guide its development, and toward which it is continually striving, giving vitality to the society". On the other hand, if I wanted to talk about America positively, I can say: "While there are deplorable racial discrimination and victimized and marginalized people in America, the important thing is that the nation is founded on very important social ideals with which to evaluate the practical situation, and to act as people's driving force for progress. In comparison, while another society might have abundant material things, it has yet to have a consensus on the minimal standards of social justice without which the society is like a ship without a compass". Neither of the above comparisons is fair, because they are "skipping the divide" in comparing the ideal of one with the practical situation of the other. In this book, realizing the unavoidable divide between ideal and reality, I have tried to avoid that fallacy by openly emphasizing the ideals in my discussions. This, to me, is more important to developing countries, because it deals with the intellectual foundation of judgments on policies and decisions. Thus, in the

Chinese case, I have been trying to show the important position that ideals occupy in Chinese heritage, even though some women in China still practice the habits of traditional social roles. I shall leave the more practical description of the Chinese society to the anthropologists and the sociologists. They are in a better position to tell us to what extent certain ideals have or have not been implement in actuality at what geographic areas, in which class of people. and under what circumstances.

With much discussion on the Chinese tradition, readers should be clear that this is only an example of the methodology I am presenting, analyzing a familiar concept and showing the important and delicate differences between two shades of meaning to a concept. The purpose of the discussion in this chapter is by no means to suggest that perhaps Confucianism or Daoism in their total traditional form should be used as a model for developing China today. There are many stifling and suffocating moral precepts in Confucianism, and much allusion to eerie phenomena of the nether land in Daoism as a religion. What I want to stress is that, although the concept and value of respecting the individual person is crucial to the intellectual foundation of a contemporary modern society, it is at least in one tradition, not tied to the Western tradition of individualism. In other words, it is not necessary that only through upholding Western individualism that people in China can come to respect the individual person. Respecting an individual person has been a value in the Chinese heritage that for thousands of years has driven Chinese history, though it is important that this respect has to be legally protected and guaranteed. When there was no legal means to protect individuals, such as during the Cultural Revolution in China, their respect, honor, physical well-being and personal properties were all trampled on.

Of course, for some, especially the young people, the discovery of Western individualism has been refreshing, and they adopt the concept whole-heartedly. But they tend to forget that the autonomous individual in the West is being loved and judged by a God who is consciously or unconsciously taken for granted as part of the Western civilization, whether one is a confessed believer or not. According to Max Weber, even capitalism was tied to the ethics of

Protestant Christianity.[51] The situation in China is entirely different. In the process of modernization, China has thrown away many important moral values, together with the stifling part of the Chinese tradition. It is no wonder that many people in China today take accumulating wealth and material things as the only aim in their lives, thinking that if the market economy is an enterprise of accumulating wealth, making money should be a logical purpose of life. Without the internal and social constraints, these Chinese "autonomous individuals" tend to be self-centered and not willing to contribute to the society as a whole, whereas according to the traditional Chinese understanding, that individual is inextricable from community and social responsibility. Therefore, the individualism upheld by the young people in China today is without roots.

To conclude, I have put forward, as one of the theses of this book, that we should understand the prevalent sociopolitical concepts from our cultural perspective. This calls for rediscovering the important values in one's culture, as many scholars in Chinese philosophy and culture are already doing today. What I also want to stress here is that, aside from gleaning one's cultural heritage, we should dissect the prevalent sociopolitical concepts themselves, and call attention to the significant impacts from the subtle different meanings of seemingly similar concepts. And each developing country will need to undergo this exercise in its own unique tradition. The conclusion of this chapter suggests that a concept of personhood has a far-reaching impact on many other concepts, and on the priority people should place on many things they do. Through the analysis of this chapter, we see that the Western concept of individualism has indeed impacted many aspects of Western, especially American, foreign policies in Asia. It has also impacted many values embedded in globalization of more recent times. In the following chapters we shall see how it has impacted other areas in Asian history over the past 2 centuries.

---

[51] Max Weber, *The Protestant Ethic and the Spirit of Capitalism*, especially pp. 2–31.

2

Human Rights and Individual Rights

Whenever we talk about "rights", we are dealing with legal matters which, in this book, will be discussed in Chapter 6. However, while we have been clarifying the concepts of respect for the individual person and individualism in Chapter 1, it is necessary to have a short chapter just following that to clarify another set of concepts relating to the impact of the last chapter, namely, on the relative importance of human rights and individual rights in developing countries. In Chapter 1, we saw that although the concept of individualism is very prominent and important in Western countries, especially America thinking and foreign policies, it is not necessarily a universal basis of respect for the individuals in all cultures. I noted that individualism has very deep roots in Western civilization, and it tends to emphasize individual liberty versus the state, thereby prioritizing political rights before all other social rights. Here, I am not so naïve as to think that to promote individual rights and liberty of the people in developing countries are the only motives, for instance, behind American foreign policies, but I wish to emphasize the values and concepts in its foreign policies that would naturally ring right and noble in the Western ears.

In this chapter, I shall suggest that because Western individualism is not necessarily a universally applicable concept, the stress on individual rights in foreign policies, especially individual political rights such as electoral rights in democratic process, may have been the stumbling block in the development of some Asian countries over the past 50 years. Historically, many developing countries, including Russia, have given top priority to individual political rights but have not had very satisfactory results. Russia, after the dissolution of the Soviet Union, embraced the Western democratic process of universal suffrage wholeheartedly under the leadership of Boris Yeltsin, and 10 years later, almost went bankrupt.

India embraced Western-type democracy in 1948 right after independence and had given its people individual political rights for almost 60 years, and yet, even with the recent boom in IT business, has not been able to eliminate widespread poverty among the masses. The Philippines is another country whose people have had individual political rights for almost 60 years. But the country has not developed economically and socially as it could have to alleviate the people's poverty and disillusionment. I shall discuss more about these countries later. These examples show how development in countries attaching more importance to individual rights rather than human rights have played out in Asian history. We are all aware that individual rights are an aspect of human rights. It is just that Western developed countries tend to put more emphasis on the individual aspect of human rights. Reading through the history of the development of the United Nations Declaration of Human Rights, we find that although the content had many stages of development, the first draft of the Declaration done in 1948 was pretty much influenced by the values of Western liberalism on individual political rights (individual vs society).

We are told by Pier Cesare Bori, during the first draft in 1948, on the wording of the first article: It stated that "All men are brothers. As human beings with the gift of reason and members of a single family, they are free and equal in dignity and rights"; the Chinese representative, P. Chang, suggested including the Confucian idea of "*ren*" beside "reason" to emphasize the human capacity for sympathy, benevolence and compassion. In the end, the final version adopted the inclusion of that idea by using the word "conscience" beside "reason" in the formulation,[1] thus adding an emphasis on human entitlement beside individual political rights. Despite that inclusion, the basic emphasis of the 1948 draft of Declaration was on civil–political liberties, as shown in the first three articles:

Article 1. All human beings are born free and equal in dignity and rights. They are endowed with reason and conscience and should act toward one another in a spirit of brotherhood.

Article 2. Everyone is entitled to all the rights and freedoms set forth in this Declaration, without distinction of any kind, such as race, color, sex, language, religion, political or other opinion, national or social origin, property, birth or other status. Furthermore, no distinction shall be made on the basis of the political, jurisdictional, or international status of the country or territory to which a person belongs, whether it be independent, trust, non-self-governing or under any other limitation of sovereignty.

Article 3. Everyone has the right to life, liberty, and security of person.

In the process of development, the United Nations Declaration of Human Rights has gradually covered the entitlement of human needs in many aspects, including considerations of culture, race, gender, and stages of societal development and the heritage belonging to all mankind. For instance, in 1970, there was an addition to the content emphasizing the considerations of the socioeconomic conditions of the developing countries; in 1979, there was an addition emphasizing women's rights; and then in 1993, there was another addition emphasizing the rights of indigenous people, together with a call for the redistribution of power, wealth, and the common heritage of mankind, such as the ecosystem, peaceful existence, and common goods on a planetary scale.[2] And it is certain

---

[1] de Bary and Tu, *Confucianism and Human Rights*, p. 41.

[2] See Sumner B. Twiss, "Constructive Framework for Discussing Confucianism and Human Rights" in *Confucianism and Human Rights*, pp. 31–32.

that, with further human sufferings hitherto not experienced, there will be a further addition of items of consideration.

Throughout the development of the UN human rights declarations, there have been disagreements between those endorsing the individualistic view and those endorsing the communitarian view of human rights. As Evelyn Kallen, alluding to S. K. Murumba's words points out, the former view insists that human dignity should not be compromised due to indefensible cultural practices, and the latter view insists that personhood is not developed in a cultural vacuum, but is shaped by the cultural particularities of one's socialization. And the debate goes on. In fact, the conflicting views resulted in two covenants in the UN: the International Covenant on Civil and Political Rights (ICCPR), and the International Covenant on Economic, Social and Cultural Rights (ICESCR).[3] It seems that to respect both the individual person's dignity and the collective human rights of different cultures is part of the spirit of the UN Human Rights Declaration. Its cardinal principle lies in the nonviolation of the rights of others, either physically or psychologically.[4] And it recognizes the rights of others who may be very different from oneself. Actually, according to Kallen, the declaration is built on the foundation of unity and cultural diversity.

> This means all human beings and all human populations can be conceptualized and studied as equals within the same comprehensive framework. This framework has no room for treatment of any human being or population as the Other. The principle of biological unity of humankind emphasizes the oneness of all human beings as members of the same human species and recognizes the close affinities between members of all human populations. The principle of cultural diversity respects the unique contribution to all humankind made by each ethno-cultural community throughout the globe.[5]

---

[3] Evelyn Kallen, *Social Inequality and Social Injustice: A Human Rights Perspective*, pp. 20–22.

[4] *Ibid*, p. 25.

[5] *Ibid*, p. 11.

Therefore, the UN Declaration of Human Rights is a very important international foundation for human rights guidelines and human rights covenants for all member states, though there are still countries challenging the universality of the Universal Declaration of Human Rights (1948). The challenges come mainly from countries objecting to those items dealing with rights in "private" spheres, such as religion, culture, the status of women, marriage, divorce, remarriage, the protection of children, family planning, and the like.[6] Those objections to reservations made on the private spheres stem from an emphasis of individual rights. And that emphasis leads to Western, especially American, foreign policies giving top priority to instituting democracy (including the embedded Western values) in developing countries.

While noting that American foreign policy gives top priority to individual rights instead of human rights, in the underdeveloped and developing countries, I am not overlooking the tremendously important humanitarian work done by many Western individuals like Albert Schweitzer in Africa and Mother Theresa in India, private organizations like Médecins sans Frontières, CARE, Oxfam, Red Cross, United Nation Organizations like UNESCO and WHO, and thousands of dedicated individual volunteers. What they did or are doing in solving human rights problems in those areas are extremely important. But still, the official foreign policies of Western nations tend to emphasize individual political rights (though the recent policies of the European Union are somewhat different).[7] Of course, it goes without saying that a country's foreign policy is usually tied to self-interest. And because of that fact with all its rationalization, it is necessary for developing countries to be aware of the embedded individualism in the programs and political prescriptions being promoted to them. Many contemporary Western thinkers are also raising objections to such over-emphasis on the autonomous individual. It shall be dealt with more in the following chapters. Here, I simply

---

[6] *Ibid*, p. 23.

[7] See Hu Yaosu, *Asian Crisis: For a Different Approach of EU's Policy Towards Asian*, especially pp. 77–80.

want to point out that to clarify this kind of confusion in important sociopolitical concepts, like human rights and individual rights, is precisely one of the intentions of this book, namely, to call attention to the different usage of such concepts, so that developing countries could be more astute in their judgment of seemingly similar concepts, while deciding what they really want as guidelines in their developments.

I have already mentioned three examples of how countries have played out historically by giving top priority to individual political rights. America's emphasis in Iraq could be another example of emphasizing individual political rights in democracy, while tremendous amount of human rights problems, such as people's personal safety, employment security, normal water and electricity supply, plus adequate medical and social care have not been addressed adequately. But the case of Iraq is complex, beginning with why the Americans and the coalition forces are there in the first place. While the unresolved inter-sectarian and inter-religious tension is already difficult enough to manage, there is the complicated explanation of the day-to-day violence, depending on one's view as to how you would call those who commit them: insurgents, or people in resistance. Indeed, the case is so complicated that it is beyond what a few pages can clarify. Nevertheless, no matter how one looks at it and whatever ulterior motives are behind the Iraq invasion, even philosophically, it is definitely a case of misplaced emphasis on individual rights.

Another illustration of misplaced emphasis of individual rights that could be cited is the criticism of China's "one-child-per-family" policy by an American human rights group. It criticized China by saying it is violating women's right to give birth in that policy. But that group ignores the fact that considering the size of China's population, China's human rights problem could never be satisfactorily solved without forcibly limiting the country's population growth, especially among the rural population. Furthermore, China's one-child-per-family policy is not a case of China's cultural belief conflicting with the UN Declaration of Human Rights, but is merely a case of simple economics to protect human rights. For instance, no matter how fast China's GDP grows, because of the size of the population, the per capita gross national income (GNI) in 2005, using the Atlas method, was around US$1740, ranked 128th in the world, and was way lower than its special administrative region, Hong Kong, which had a per capita GNI of around $27,670. Even by the purchasing power parity method, China's per capita GNI was still only around $6600, and ranked 107th in the world.[8] It is obvious that with the size of China's population, not to have a national family-planning policy is just economically not justifiable. The criticism of China's family-planning policy by that human rights group is another example of putting individual rights above human rights in the wrong place and at the wrong time.

There are borderline cases of human rights and individual rights, like the debates on euthanasia and abortion. But such extremely emotionally charged ethical problems, as well as complicated debates like that on gay marriage, should meaningfully belong to a stage of development in which the society is fine-tuning the human entitlement, and not to one where parts of the population are still living on bare subsistence without adequate medical care and minimum education for the children, or where the population is growing at a rate that would challenge the minimum distribution of social resources. The above examples are ample to indicate some of the misplaced priorities on individual rights and misconceptions about individual rights and human rights.

I should clarify that the discussion from here onward will be limited to the context of an open and pluralistic society and not to one with a tyrannical ruler about which will be discussed in Chapter 5. Here, I merely want to emphasize the discussion on the clarification of human rights. First, we have to inquire into what it is to be human, so as to fully understand what human beings are entitled to, and then to assert what are their rights. Many scholars are now holding widespread discussions and debates on such issues. For our discussion, however, we shall merely point out that whatever human entitlements eventually emerge from the discussions and debates,

---

[8] See 2006 World Bank figures for China (2005), and US Department of State figures for Hong Kong.

they should at least include those entitlements germinating from the following existential human yearnings. In Chapter 6, for example, I shall point out that the respect for the individual person, freedom, and equality are all basic human yearnings. They are not inventions of any culture, but are basic yearnings of all human beings. Without exception, all human beings yearn for an environment that allows "self-respect" and "freedom". And with a bit of reasoning in reciprocity, we can understand that other human beings also have the same yearnings, thus leading us to the conviction of "equality". And if we use the traditional Chinese view of the concept of the unity of man and nature,[9] for example, we shall also support the 1993 amendment to the UN Declaration of Human Rights on the ecosystem. The very fact that, with the exception of some religious practices and cultural customs, the United Nations could have an internationally accepted Universal Declaration of Human Rights, shows that there are specifications of human entitlements that go to the very foundation of human existence. Ronald Niezen puts it this way: "The human rights system is a legally-formulated moral code that somehow appeals to spiritual sensibilities".[10] What is said here shows that human rights cover a very wide range of human entitlements. When applied to sociopolitical concepts, we should at least have respect for the individual person, freedom, and equality as basic universal human entitlements. What is important to our discussion is to affirm that an individual person, being a member of humanity, much of his/her rights are in the domain of human rights, and not necessarily rights belonging to a unique autonomous individual. On the other hand, as we have seen in the last chapter, the emphasis on the entitlement of humanity in general is not necessarily to smother the respect for an individual person or to ignore the rights of an individual, if seen through a concept of personhood discussed there.

Translated into political entitlement, each individual person of a society is to be treated as a citizen of the society, entitled to have

---

[9] See Sumner B. Twiss, "Constructive Framework for Discussing Confucianism and Human Rights" in *Confucianism and Human Rights*, p. 32.

[10] *A World Beyond Differences*, p. 87.

the status of an honorable member, sharing with others the common goal of the society, and having all the privileges within that society that lead to an identity with the community he/she belongs to. Here, I am using the minimum specification of a definition of citizenship given by Daniel Weinstock.[11] Using this concept of citizenship, the state is to protect all its citizens' entitlement in terms of the basic human yearnings discussed earlier. In protecting the rights of its citizens, the basic rule-of-thumb a state usually uses is the general utilitarian principle of serving the greatest good of the greatest number of people. This is workable as a minimum, but we should not overlook the risk of what J. S. Mill called the "tyranny of the majority", especially as we become aware that there are different sectors in a society, each having their own subcultures, values, interests, and needs, forming their unique rights in a pluralistic society. Thus, while emphasizing the importance of satisfying human rights of the greatest number of citizens, the state must also be sensitive to the needs and entitlements belonging to the citizens of different sectors of the society. To reduce the risk of smothering the interests and needs of minority groups, some people suggested that the only way minority interests and needs could be voiced and protected was through the forming of small autonomous groups. That may be a natural thing to do, but they still have to work within the context of the state's governance. To fulfill the functions of voicing their minority views and needs, they have to be acknowledged and legalized by the state. And the state needs to acknowledge and listen to their interests and needs to preserve social unity. This is especially necessary for the developing countries, because most of the Asian countries are multi-racial and multi-religious countries, while national unity is of utmost importance to development.

Secondly, the very fact that some subgroups exist, whether on gender, neighborhood or ethnic grounds, because of their common needs and culture or values, are not deliberately formed but exist as

---

[11] See "Citizenship and Pluralism" in *Blackwell Guide to Social and Political Philosophy*, p. 244.

facts. Thus, recognizing them as citizens of the society and acknowledging their voices and needs will enhance their sense of belonging to that society. For instance, as mentioned in the Introduction of this book, China pays particular attention to the voices and needs of the 55 minority nationalities other than the majority Han nationality. And in the recent 20 some years, there have been special policies toward the "groups with weak resources"[12] like the disabled. There are policies providing suitable employment in professions in various forms of arts and performances. When migrant workers have become a sizable group, there are policies to take care of the primary education of their children in the cities, though the enforcement of the policies on their living conditions and delinquent back-pays have not been too satisfactory. Nevertheless, by paying careful attention to the voices and needs of the minority groups or the civil societies, the state can attempt to satisfy their group rights, together with their individual rights, thereby enhancing their sense of belonging to the community they live in.

There are also minority groups deliberately formed because of common values, interests, and needs. Some of these, like religious groups, are groups with private interests and private needs, though some other groups could have general significance to the public, such as a small social–conscious group expressing concerns of social problems, like the children of migrant workers left at home, or the major water pollution problem in China. The seriousness of these issues was actually made known through the attention of small groups. Some people fear that the voices of these small groups might fragment the society. But as long as they do not have the intention to do so, they are legitimate and useful groups to prevent the "tyranny of the majority". Thus, it shows that by merely having a democratically elected government and relying on regional representatives to redress the interests and needs of their constituents, does not necessarily provide a total solution to the kind of problems discussed here, because the local governments

---

[12] 弱势群体.

could be a part of the problems. I shall address that at another place in this book.

Parenthetically, I notice that among all the discussions of this subject under consideration, there has been much neglect of the contributions and effects of the Internet in this information age. The fact that Hyde Park Corner in London has become less important nowadays is because people can voice their ideas and needs through the Internet (though there are still people using the soap-box there to express their views. However, the spectators nowadays are taking the occasion more as entertainment than any serious dialogues). In China, the prime minister's office today has a group of staff collecting, categorizing, and analyzing thousands of letters written electronically to the prime minister, as he has publicly encouraged that. Granted, voicing opinion is different from taking action, the different media in the information age have nevertheless made it much easier for the government to be aware of the ideas and needs of its citizens, whether in the majority or in the minority sectors, thereby making it much easier and more effective for the government to implement programs addressing those interests and needs. That the Chinese government's attention was drawn to ameliorate the problem of migrant workers' children left at home (some estimate them to be in the millions) and the water pollution problem are cases in point.

Thus, after understanding what is crucial for human entitlement, we shall see, first of all, we need to have an independent and effective state to attack problems in the neglect of human rights. Secondly, to solve these problems, much human and economic resources are needed from the state. Thirdly, in today's globalized world, a strong state (not necessarily authoritarian) is needed to maintain sovereignty without being victimized by external forces. Therefore, coming back to the priority of developing countries, it is evident that the state has a heavy responsibility to guarantee a minimum degree of human entitlement, especially in improving the physical environment, medical care, education, social well-being which all need government funding and that in turn means a critical need for a concerted effort to drive economic growth. For instance, because of the resources from the economic growth in China, it is able to reduce the number of people under the poverty line from 250 million in 1978 (30% of rural population) to 42 million in 1998 (4.6% of rural population).[13] Whichever way one wants to take the statistics, they show that the ability to drastically reduce poverty in China is related directly to its economic growth.

A study by Mary Dowell-Jones in 2004 about improving the effectiveness of implementing the UN Declaration of Human Rights emphasizes precisely the importance of economic consideration of a country. The study is about the ICIESCR (Internal Covenant on Economic, Social and Cultural Rights) which is "at the center of the international human rights legal order, forming part of the international Bill of Rights alongside the Universal Declaration of Human Rights (UDHR) and the International Covenant on Civil and Political Rights (ICCPR)".[14] This agency deals with the legal obligation of member states on the covenants they have made in relation to implementing human rights in their countries. The study shows that the work of the agency has not been effective since its founding in 1985, because its legal order has not taken into consideration the economic context of the countries that the covenant deals with. For instance, Article 2(1) of CIESCR specifically states[15]:

(a) Objectives set must be affordable given current means; and
(b) Objectives set must not be such as to compromise the future ability of the economy to achieve those rights.

But the ICESCR committee members, except for one economist, are all lawyers. Thus, in carrying out the work of the covenant, the economic aspects have often been neglected. This leads Dowell-Jones to suggest: "The implementation of Covenant standards requires a certain allocation of participation in, and the fruits of, economic activity for each individual within a broader framework of

---

[13] *United Nations Development Program: "Poverty in China"* Data updated in December, 2001.

[14] Mary Dowell-Jones, *Contextualizing the International Covenant on Economic, Social and Cultural Rights*, p. 1.

[15] *Ibid*, p. 6.

efficient macroeconomic organization which guarantees the resources for continuing progressive improvement of the standards".[16]

This means that, in order for the protection of the rights to be effective in a particular country, there must be a socioeconomic foundation in the first place, and then a recognition that the economic situation of a country is also fluid. As Dowell-Jones, quoting Galbraith, says: "The greatest error in economics is in seeing economy as a stable, immutable structure".[17] In conclusion, Dowell-Jones again stresses that "as a contextual, historically-situated document, the import of the Covenant of Guarantees must be subject to continued reassessment in light of the ebb and flow of the fluid relationship of state and individual within the parameters of the evolving economic conditions and needs".[18]

From the above recent review of the effectiveness of a UN agency in implementing the legal order of human rights covenant, we see that a carefully studied conclusion concurs with the idea that economic growth and the condition of the economic resources of a country, as well as implementing human rights programs on the basis of that economic information are crucial to the success of the work on evaluating the human rights covenant. Some believe that developing countries should institute democracy first, because it would drive economic growth. They believe that once a country has democracy, the elected body would naturally improve the lives of people. But history as cited above tells us very strongly that this is not necessarily the case. And according to many studies, there seems to be little correlation between economic growth and democracy. According to one study, the establishment of individual political rights at low level may stimulate economic growth. But once a moderate amount of democracy has been obtained, a further expansion of individual rights may even lead to negative impact on economic growth.[19] So, on the question of correlation between democracy and economic development, Robert Cassen

---

[16] *Ibid*, p. 6.

[17] *Ibid*, p. 7.

[18] *Ibid*, p. 7.

[19] Li Xiaobing, "Democracy and Economic Growth: A Case Study" in *Taiwan in the Twenty First Century*, p. 140f.

notes that "…closer scrutiny bears out that some non-democratic regimes have done well, others have ruined their economies, and the same is true for democracies. In general, there is no correlation".[20]

In 1995, a survey was conducted around the area of Beijing, China by Daniel Dowel, Allen Carlson, and Shen Mingming. Those surveyed were asked, anonymously, to make only one preference among the following: (1) Individual freedom; (2) Public order; (3) Fair administration of justice; (4) Social equality; (5) Political democracy; and (6) National peace and prosperity. The result showed that, across all age and gender groups, over 44.9% of people surveyed were in favor of national peace and prosperity, whereas only 13% and 10% preferred fair administration of justice and social equality, respectively. The result indicated that:

(1) There is a pressure for a more "liberal society" with more "private space for individuals".
(2) Income has no effect on preference for democracy or personal freedom.

Those conducting the survey got the impression that people desired to be left alone by the government.[21] Another set of surveys done in 551 villages in China between 1993 and 1994 reported by Shi Tianjian showed that in pushing for democracy, the local officials played a key role. So, they had to analyze the relationship not only between economic development and democracy, but also between the state and society. The report showed that economic development might make it difficult, if not impossible, for village officials to co-opt their constituents in the future. Thus, while economic development would both increase ordinary people's ability to participate in politics and make the incumbent officials more difficult to co-opt constituents, it will change their attitude toward elections.[22] Both surveys in China concurred with Robert Cassen's

---

[20] Robert Cassen, "Democracy and Development" in *Democracy, Human Rights and Economic Development*, p. 27.

[21] Zhao Suisheng (ed.), *China and Democracy*, pp. 189–192.

[22] *Ibid*, pp. 244–247.

observation that there seems to be no necessary connection between economic growth or wealth and the preference for political participation or democracy at the early stages of development. All in all, good political governance seems to be important to economic growth. But the histories of some Asian countries tell us that democracy does not necessarily lead to good governance. The elected body could be very conscientious, hard-working, and all-caring, but then it could also turn out to be a private club of the privileged few enjoying each other's homily in the parliament or congress, bickering over their internal differences, and not paying much attention to the rights of the general masses.

I shall emphasize later that democracy is a complex concept. Western democracy comes with many embedded values. If we dissect the concept, and take away some of the values which are irrelevant for the developing countries in Asia, we shall need to inject positive local values into the skeleton of the democratic process to make it work for the welfare of the people in Asia. Without a value system for public good, the candidates seeking to be elected may use all sorts of devious methods to defame the opponent, to side-track the important issues, and even bribe the innocent public or create incidents to dramatize their valiant image in order to be elected. And once they are elected and their goals achieved, they soon tend to forget the mandate given by the people. This is to say, promoting individual rights in democracy as the number one priority when the basic entitlements of human rights have not been established, or the social well-being of the citizens is not in the minds of the elected, the consequence just do not play out well historically.

Now what has been said about human rights problems in developing countries has been compounded by globalization. This raises the question of whether a country at the developing stage needs to be a strong state (not necessarily an authoritarian state) to protect itself from the forces of globalization, and whether its human rights problems may become uncontrollable. Much has been written and much debated on the benefits and ills caused by globalization. For instance, according to Natalia Dinello and Lyn Squire, the Nobel Laureate economist, Joseph Stiglitz (President of the Bill Clinton

Council of Economic Advisors and Chief Economist of World Bank) thought that international financial institutions have failed to alleviate poverty and stimulate economic growth in the era of globalization. His colleague at Columbia University, Jagdish Bhahwati, proposed that globalization had benefited emerging markets by creating virtuous economic cycles of faster economic growth, and in some cases, had improved the lot of women and children in developing countries. George Soros criticized the fundamentalism in roles played by the international financial and trade institutions by not serving the poor and improving development, while New York Times foreign affairs columnist Thomas Friedman described globalization as "a lasting phenomenon — an integrated system that has replaced the cold war system — goes beyond economics to highlight the tension between the integrated modern world and the age-old forces of culture, geography, tradition and community".[23]

I do not think anybody queries the undeniable fact that the world is becoming more integrated through globalization. The world nowadays is more interconnected through information technology, computerization, and the Internet and public media, through more worldwide trading, and a more prevalent and easier flow of capital and finance. However, to be internationally interconnected is not a new phenomenon. For instance, there were the ocean route and overland route of the Silk Road to and from China for international trade and intercultural exchanges hundreds of years ago. Likewise in Europe, as Dani Rodrik points out, "The world economy was possibly even more integrated at the height of the gold standard in the late 19th century than it is now".[24] And nobody denies that globalization has brought benefits in stimulating trade and economic growth, reducing poverty and contributing to economic and political stability in some countries. But the trouble is that it, at the same time, has also brought devastating consequences in some other countries by introducing economic vulnerability, job insecurity, worsening inequality, and eroding national sovereignty. All depending on their stages of

---

[23] Natalia Dinello and Lyn Squire (eds.), *Globalization and Equality*, p. xii.
[24] "Has Globalization Gone too Far?" in *Global Transformations Reader*, p. 381.

development, economic competitiveness and institutional flexibility, globalization has brought different effects, depending on whether the countries are strong enough economically and politically to withstand the various harmful forces of globalization in order to take advantage of its benefits. This shows how important it is for the developing countries to have national sovereignty and the ability to choose whether to resist or welcome the forces of globalization. If they are to welcome it, then they should choose which aspects of it they should welcome.

To illustrate this point further, we have to examine the role of the major players in the globalization process. The phenomena we are facing today are really something that happened in the final decades of the 20th century. Robert Gilpin notes that "The recent global economic integration has been the result of major changes in trade flows, of activities of multinational corporations and the development in international finance".[25] Thus, globalization cannot be disassociated from the growing influence of international financial organizations such as IMF and the World Bank, which by themselves, should be ideal organizations for the support of development. But unfortunately, as it turns out, these organizations, based on their theory of neoliberalism, have over powering influence on weaker and smaller states to push for less state intervention in a country's economy, to deregulate central controls, and to liberalize the goods market, labor market, financial, and capital markets, leaving many states with less control of their own economies. Many countries, indeed, have objected their predicament. For example, after the 1997 Southeast Asia financial crisis, IMF had rescue packages for the affected countries. But its conditions for structural and institutional reforms were entirely unacceptable to those countries,[26] and they were modified only after public protests in South Korea and Thailand, and rioting in Indonesia.[26]

When globalization shifted into high gear, some less developed countries found themselves without any control, facing the onslaught of worldwide competition. Barbara Harriss-White notes that: "The very idea that the economy can or must be separated from the political sphere is part of the ideological underpinning

---

[25] "Nation-state in the Global Economy" in *Ibid*, p. 350.
[26] See Chia Siow Yue, "East Asia" in *Globalization and Equality*, p. 108.

of globalization".[27] And according to her, globalization creates threats and insecurities physically, economically, and socially in developing countries. So, "When developing states with fragile institutional architectures deregulate, their weak capacity to protect poor people weakens yet more. Many kinds of instability result — social unrest, forced migration, flow of refugees, robbery and armed conflict".[28] Robert Gilpin concurs with this view and says,

> Thus, although economic globalization has increased the latitude of governments to pursue expansionary economic policies through borrowing excessively abroad, such serious financial crises of the postwar era as the Mexican crisis 1994–1995, the 1997 East Asian financial crisis, and the disturbing collapse of the Russian ruble in August 1998 demonstrated the huge and widespread risks associated with such practices.[29]

Although recently, there have been a "post-Washington Consensus" modification of the policies, and global governance requirements of IMF and the World Bank aimed not necessarily to benefit particular advanced capitalist states and just to strengthen the global capitalist system, it is still exposing the small and weak countries to, and putting them at, the mercy of the logic of raw capitalism.

The above discussion reveals the complexity of human rights problems in developing countries confronting globalization. It points further to the issues of priorities and self-determination. For the developing countries, solving human rights problems should definitely be the top priority, but there may be external forces saying otherwise. And to be able to say no to external disagreeable forces requires a strong sovereign state. And its economy also needs to be a nationally controlled macroeconomic so that the human rights problems within each country could be disassociated from the push and pull of external forces. Theoretically, there should be international dialogues and negotiations on what economic policies to implement by the international financial organizations while making

---

[27] Barbara Harrriss-White, *Globalization and Insecurity*, p. 2.
[28] *Ibid*, p. 6.
[29] "Nation-state in the Global Economy" in *Global Transformations Reader*, p. 357.

loans to developing countries, but realistically, the smaller and weaker nations just do not have the negotiating leverage. The United States, for example, could afford to operate effectively in domestic affairs by a 'small government', because before the Iraq war and the sub-prime debacle, it could influence the global currency market through the US dollars; and influence the global currency market through its major international institutions; the global business through its multi-nationals; the global geo-politics through its technological might and world-wide military presence; and the global intellectual inclinations through its multi-facet media.

All in all, what people have learned from the experience of developing countries in the last 3 decades is that there is a necessary role for the state to play in effective development, and it does not have to be an authoritarian state. Ha-Joon Chang concludes that developing countries need a selective industrial and trade policy to guide their economic development, and that policy requires the support of institutions such as "the bureaucracy, state-owned enterprises, institution for controls of financial flows, and intermediate institutions such as deliberation councils and industrial associations".[30] In view of the discussion here, it seems, while democracy that gives individual political rights is ultimately important to a country, it should certainly not be a priority for developing countries if there are pressing human rights problems to address, especially amidst the fierce international economic competition. For instance, it is difficult to envision that agreements can be easily reached on programs of human rights in a democracy like that of India which had 328 parties taking part in the first 10 elections during the 1951–1991 period, and 209 parties in elections even as late as 1996. Concluding about the coalition among the parties in the Indian parliament, Francine Frankel says: The "unstable and/or internally divided coalitions operating within a 'minimum agreed program' slowed down the decision making process, taking its greatest toll on implementation of second stage economic reforms".[31] And those reforms

---

[30] Chang Ha-Joon, *Globalization, Economic Development and the Role of the State*, pp. 328–329.

[31] Francine Frankel, *India's Political Economy*, p. 630.

were crucial for the reduction of poverty and miseries among the greater masses of India. This also means that the emphasis on specific items of human rights and the priorities for implementation are relative to different countries at different junctures in their historical development. For some countries, to have a roof above one's head, clean water and food on the table, medicine for the sick, and minimum education for the young might be the most urgent human rights needs. For others, it might be employment, social security, and more thorough medical and educational programs. For still others, it might be legal protection of the citizens' rights, universal health care and higher education, the establishment of cultural identity and dignity of the people. Some of these might be social rights and not political rights, human rights in general and not individual rights. If we can compress history, we have witnessed similar urgency of fulfilling human rights even in developed countries. For example, when there is a catastrophic natural calamity, a society has to suspend individual rights temporarily for the sake of human rights to guarantee food, water, medicine, lodging, public order, and safety, as in New Orleans, America after the Hurricane Katrina in September, 2005.

It is clear from the discussion of this chapter that to prioritize individual political rights in a democratic process when human rights problems are still too widespread in developing countries, is to put the cart before the horse. I shall deal with individual rights more in relation to personal freedom and political rights in later chapters. This chapter only wants to stress the fact, as Asian history of the last 50 years has already told us, that a hasty emphasis on promoting individual political rights might not necessarily guarantee an implementation of minimum human rights. To take care of the problems of human rights first and then the problems of individual rights gradually, however slow the process might be, will eventually play out better in history. And this short chapter also wants to clarify the concepts of human rights and individual rights. In the Western world, due to its belief in individualism, individual rights has often been used interchangeably with human rights, and the consequences have been, at best misleading, and in worst cases, even detrimental to development in Asia.

Chapter 3

Freedom from Want and
Freedom of Choice

"Freedom" in this chapter is limited to discussion on freedom of human activities in the sociopolitical spheres, and not in the metaphysical sphere, such as free will versus determinism.

The yearning for freedom is not a new thing; nor is it a unique Western concept. All human beings seek freedom from bondage, and quest for spontaneity and creativity. As Benedetto Croce puts it:

> "...freedom may be regarded as the force that creates history — indeed this is so truly its real and proper function that one might say, in a sense somewhat different from the Hegelian, that history is the history of freedom. In fact, everything the human being does and creates is done or created freely — actions, political institutions, religious conceptions, scientific theories, the production of poetry and art, technical inventions, instruments for increasing wealth and power".[1]

All are familiar with stories of lovers thirsting for freedom from social pressure as portrayed by Shakespeare's tragedy "Romeo and Juliet" and the modern musical "West Side Story" that tells of the tragic love between a white American boy and a Puerto Rican girl

---

[1] "The Roots of History" in *Freedom and Its Meaning*, pp. 28–29.

in New York City. There were similar stories in the Chinese tradition. An example would be the ancient story of "Butterfly Lovers",[2] in which two lovers were kept apart because of different social backgrounds, and in line with Chinese belief in the unity of Man and Nature, they only consummated their love when they later turned into butterflies. And the yearning for freedom can also be seen in the following famous Chinese poems from the eighth century. In both poems, the poets sought freedom from the worldly hassle of wealth, fame, and officialdom and opted to embrace nature with a simple life of solitude:

AUTUMN EVENING IN THE MOUNTAIN

(By Wang Wei)

After fresh rain in mountains bare
Autumn permeates evening air.
Among pine-trees bright moonbeams peer;
O'er crystal stones flows water clear.
Bamboos whisper of washer-maids;
Lotus stirs when fishing boat wades.
Though fragrant spring may pass away,
Still here's the place for you to stay.[3]

SITTING ALONE IN FACE OF PEAK JINGTING

(By Li Bai)

All birds have flown away, so high;
A lonely cloud drifts on, so free.
Gazing on Mount Jingting, nor I
Am tired of him, nor he of me.[4]

---

[2] 梁山伯与祝英台.
[3] 王维 '山居秋暝' *Bilingual Edition 300 Tang Poems*, p. 90.
[4] 李白 '坐敬亭山' *Bilingual Edition 300 Tang Poems*, p. 180.

Perhaps to some, the metaphors used in these poems are not obviously about the poets' yearning for political freedom. It might be true but, nevertheless, the poets were seeking for some kind of freedom. First, they highlighted the traditional Chinese concept of the unity of Man and Nature. As Thomas Berry, in expounding Chinese spirituality, puts it "…The Chinese discovered a more intimate presence of the universe and the individual to each other … this might be called a doctrine of humanity.[5] Second, political freedom is not the only kind of freedom. Whatever kind of freedom one wants to read into the poems, they implied that the poets desired emancipation from the worldly hassles and bustles, and yearned for a quiet life in tune with nature.

So, freedom is a natural and basic human yearning. Our freedom may be bound by political powers, family authorities, social pressures, moral constraints, health conditions, educational limitations, economic realities or physical disabilities.

Some bondages we can break by establishing political and legal institutions thereby gaining freedom of political choice; and some we can break by developing social and economic programs to provide basic needs of decent human existence and also human means of empowerment; thereby gaining "freedom from want". Admittedly, in actual development, the processes of providing "freedom of choice" and "freedom from want" cannot be entirely separated, but have to be promoted concurrently; at every step of promoting economic and social programs to solve poverty, as well as medical, and educational problems, there is concurrently a need to satisfy some people's demand for freedom of choice through participating in understanding and accepting the required moral guidance, legal regulations, and economic mechanism in running those programs smoothly. And at every step of promoting people's freedom of choice, there has to be concurrently a need to provide freedom from want in improving their educational standard, economic well-being, and political awareness. Here again, it is a matter of priority. Usually, resources are limited, be they

---

[5] Thomas de Berry, "Individualism and Holism in Chinese Tradition" in *Confucian Spirituality*, p. 49.

financial or qualified personnel. Where a government puts most of its resources, and in what order to allocate its resources, depends on which of the freedoms it emphasizes. So, even though the development of the two freedoms taking place concurrently and the demands for two forms of freedoms are made concurrently, there is a difference in emphasis and order in execution at a particular point in time. From the implication of the discussions in Chapter 1, we see that it is the influence of individualism in American foreign policy that puts priority on the freedom of political choice, often at the expense of the urgently needed programs to provide freedom from want, which in a certain understanding of the concept of personhood, and with a certain understanding of freedom as, I shall momentarily suggest, an emancipation from poverty of what is vital to the human spirit, really acknowledges a profound respect for the individual.

Besides, history has shown us that it is much more important to first solve the problem of "freedom from want" than to satisfy the "freedom of choice" for developing countries. Those developing countries that rushed into solving the problems of freedom of political choice in their initial stage of development without the financial resources to provide freedom from want tend to end up in stagnation, thus limiting even more of the resources to alleviate the social and economic problems of the general masses in their societies.

Freedom of choice, especially political choice, will naturally come at a certain stage of development. But to establish the economic, moral, social, and legal systems that are necessary for a political system that could afford people the freedom of choice, takes philosophical perceptiveness, professional knowledge, understanding of one's culture, political astuteness, legal enforcement and, most important of all, time which may be years or decades. And a developing country in the early stages just cannot afford to ignore solving the problem of freedom from want in the meantime. It is obvious that without the satisfaction of freedom from want of a more sophisticated level, it would be difficult even to have the conditions just mentioned to have a sound and effective political system in which freedom of political choice could be practiced effectively.

Francine Frankel's analysis of India is very telling. Because of its IT development in the late 1980s, India had an economic growth that peaked from 1994 to 1997 (1994/1995: 7.3% and 1996/1997: 7.8%), but growth rate sharply declined after those years to 4.8%, 6.5%, 6.1%, and 5.2% in 1997/1998, 1998/1999, 1999/2000, and 2000/2001, respectively.[6] She further says that "India's economic structure remains typical of low-income nations, which are poor precisely because they have not been able to provide productive work for a growing labour force in agriculture...".[7] And she continues:

> "Had earlier governments [of India] invested more on education, health facilities and rural development, and had they implemented programs for land redistribution, community development and agrarian reorganization as the institutional rationale for self-reliant industrialization during the first three years of the five-year plans, rising rural income and expanding domestic market could have been created over time that would also have prevented India from missing the "industrial revolution". It would also have provided a much more favourable environment for a high level of sustained growth after the introduction of reforms".[8]

In a later chapter on democracy, I shall deal with this issue more in detail. What is said here is enough to distinguish clearly between the two kinds of freedom and to stress the importance of putting priority in satisfying freedom from want in developing countries.

Some may question that a government would have the inclination to institute sound economic and social programs to alleviate the plight of the people if that government is not elected by the people. But as we have just discussed, in the last chapter and this one, the history of Asia in the last 50 years has not shown any correlation between people's freedom of political choice and economic growth of that country. Neither has there been a correlation between officials elected by the people and their compassion to alleviate the plight of the people who put them in power. So, it is questionable that an elected government would necessarily have the inclination and urgency to ameliorate the miseries of the general masses. While democracy might be a good thing, and its simple form could possibly be

---

[6] See Francine Frankel, *India's Political Economy*, pp. 598–599.

[7] *Ibid*, p. 611.

[8] *Ibid*, p. 615.

practiced in a small village, a full democracy with people exercising their freedom of choice takes sophistication of the voting public and the above-mentioned social infrastructure to make it work in a country of size. In fact, without that infrastructure in place, democracy does not even work in small villages where there are dominant or influential figures in the villages to resist change. This again is borne out in India during the administration of Indira Gandhi. Although all the command and the Congress Party were under her control, the government had no administrative apparatus at the grass-root level to carry out her agricultural reforms. In the end, the programs at the village level were directed by the rural elites who were actually the leading members of the dominant landowning caste. Therefore, the program to solve rural poverty naturally did not make any progress.[9]

Of course, as a country develops, its people will demand more and more sophisticated freedoms, including such things as higher education, more comprehensive medical care, more social mobility, more personal dignity and protection of their rights and property, more cultural identity and enrichment, more current events information, and more voice in political decisions of the society. When these conditions are not there, or people have a confused notion of freedom, the emphasis of freedom of choice might even hurt the implementation of the freedom of want. For instance, because of the tradition of individualism, there has been an overemphasis of the individual's political freedom (liberty), making the freedom of political choice, a top priority in Western foreign policies. However, in reality, beside people's demand for political freedom, there are demands for other kinds of freedoms: traveling to where they prefer; residing where they wish; doing what interests them and what is most enriching and fulfilling to them; loving and marrying whom they please; owning whatever they cherish; as well as searching for whatever they want in intellectual and spiritual spheres. Western liberalism tends to lump those freedoms just listed all under the rubric of political freedom, meaning politically allowable in certain historical authoritarian societies; whereas they are actually freedoms in relation

---

[9] *Ibid*, p. 547.

to the social environment, and not necessarily to the political environment. They should be called social freedoms. In this sense, the satisfaction of "freedom from want" is important for developing countries, because its satisfaction would provide the resources that could practically allow social freedoms. This becomes especially clear when we see that people's "wants" are not limited to basic physical subsistence, but also more sophisticated needs; that is, aside from those social needs listed above, there are also psychological needs for identity and dignity, and cultural needs of lifting human spirituality. Parenthetically, according to some surveys, the need for political choice may not even be an important one among other needs in the lives and minds of people. I shall come to that at a later point. In any case, for our discussion here, I have shown that aside from the distinction of "freedom from want" and "freedom of choice", there is also a distinction between freedom of political choice and freedom of social choice, and there are even different aspects of social freedom. It seems clear, then, that it is a mistake to prioritize the freedom of political choice unconditionally in the developing countries. To understand the nuances of the issue, we have to probe further into the concept of freedom.

Freedom implies emancipation from a plight such as poverty; and in another dimension, it implies emancipation from some constraints like legal regulations or other people's conflicting demands. If freedom from want belongs to the former dimension (emancipation from poverty) and freedom of political choice belongs to an aspect of the latter dimension (emancipation from constraints), there exists a great gap between the two in urgency for developing country. Besides, freedom of political choice is concerned with emancipation from only one of many kinds of constraints, some urgent and some not so urgent depending on the values held by a society and the historical circumstances.

Let us first look at emancipation from one of the dire plights of developing countries; say, poverty. Of course, the sense of poverty that comes to mind readily is the lack of physical conditions for healthy subsistence like a roof over one's head, clean water and food on the table, warm clothes on one's body, minimum medical care, and rudimentary education. But poverty in a deeper sense means much more than that. It also means a lack of something very important to a person; such as personal respect, identity, and dignity. Only when a person has fulfilled that "lacking" can we say that he/she has the sense of freedom that everyone yearns for as mentioned in the beginning of this chapter.

There are many ways people feel "lacking". And there are also different ways for different people to interpret a "lacking". Take the phenomenon of money for example. To the multi-billionaires, money is a symbol; to those in the financial businesses and the capital market, money is a commodity, but to the ordinary wage and salary earners, it is a means to gain freedom. There is a Chinese saying: "Money is not all powerful, but without it one is rendered powerless".[10] That means, to many people, money is a means of gaining personal freedom from want. With it, one can buy what one likes, go where one wants, be what one inclines; and might have a peace of mind that is above one's material and existing state of affairs. Lest we forget, what Americans feared during the 1929 depression was also more than economic losses. David Fischer concludes: "It created a new sense of social urgency in 1929, when the market crashed and the economy fell in the depth of a great depression. The collapse of the economy was perceived not only as an economic crisis but as a fundamental threat to liberty and freedom".[11]

In a way, for those who already have sufficient money for a comfortable living, freedom mean emancipation from something else; like boredom, a lack of personal esteem or a lack of fulfillment of personhood. Anybody who has any knowledge about management of people in business knows that the staff want not only economic remuneration but also personal recognition, opportunity for creativity, a sense of accomplishment, and a sense of satisfaction with the working environment, including with co-workers and the company culture. In other words, what people need more than

---

[10] 钱不是万能，但没有钱万万不能.
[11] David Fischer, *Liberty and Freedom*, p. 478.

economic security is a freedom from the humdrum and a need to fulfill that vital dimension of personhood.

What is that vital dimension of personhood? Here, I owe much to David Levine and S. Abu Turab Rizvi for their discussion of poverty, work, and freedom. Although, I disagree with their post-modernist and individualistic solution to the problem; especially in the end, when they emphasized personal creativity to the exclusion of common community values, moral teaching at schools, and the state's intervention in every type of personal creative endeavors, leaving the state's relationship with its citizens as only one of stewardship, I have however, gained much insight from their discussions on the vital dimension of personhood. I shall come to this post-modernist version of sociopolitical philosophy later. At this point, I think their use of a psychoanalytic study of a person could be usefully applied to our discussion of the group psyche of a society in developing countries. According to Levine and Rizvi, our vital dimension of personhood is derived from personal fulfillment and well-being that comes from "...a state of finding comfort in our experience of ourselves" and "our ability to find comfort in the experience of the self depends on our ability to make a positive emotional investment in the self".[12] It is a development from within oneself, rather than from the external environment. And that development is an emancipation from life's "poverty", which is not measured by a lack of wealth, but by what we are or are not capable of. In this sense, according to Levine and Rizvi, "Poverty is implied in the ascription of a denigrated identity".[13] The vital dimension of personhood comes down to personal identity, which Levine and Rizvi, quoting Erikson,[14] say that it has at least the following five qualities:

1. Self-awareness.
2. Continuity of being across time.

---

[12] Levine and Rizvi, *Poverty, Work and Freedom*, p. 56.

[13] *Ibid*, p. 56.

[14] *Ibid*, p. 60; Discusson of identity from: Erickson, E., *Identity and Life Cycle*.

3.   The involvement of meaning in a connected life experience.
4.   Finiteness of boundedness; realizing what we are and what we are not.
5.   Recognition by others, sharing with others and connecting to others.

When we move from the discussion of a person to a society, I find all the above factors applicable to the vital dimension of a people in relation to their identity of their past, present, and future, namely, national and cultural identity. In other words, when we talk about people's identity in developing countries, first of all, we mean that the people of those countries must have an awareness of themselves as a consolidated and integrated people. Second, they must be aware of where they come from, where they have been and how they have come together; namely their history. Third, they must be aware of the meaning and value of their prolonged group experience; namely their culture. Fourth, they must be aware of what makes them who they are; namely their unique distinctiveness. Fifth, they must be aware of their membership in a larger family of countries globally; namely their rights and obligations in international affairs.

This means, when we talk about freedom from want in the developing countries, we are not only talking about the elimination of physical poverty and the satisfaction of basic subsistence, but also emancipating people from the poverty of lacking self-respect, cultural identity, national dignity, social freedoms, and international justice. What I suggested a few paragraphs back about the need for the development of social, economic infrastructure, and sophisticated "freedom from want" before satisfying the freedom of political choice, I meant also that there was the need to have the structure to emancipate people from poverty in the areas of identity. So, "freedom from want" has to take precedence in development such that when the time comes to practice political choice, the people would have the identity with the country to vote responsibly and have the self-respect and dignity to monitor the political progress responsibly; and those elected officials would also have the identity with the country's history and culture, and have the compassion toward the plight of the people making all that their vital business to govern effectively, efficiently, and responsibly. It is no wonder, when people in some Asian democratic countries do not have those identities, the voting public tend to view exercising their right to vote as the end of their political responsibilities, and the elected officials also tend to view being elected as the end of their responsibility to their mandate, leaving the country's urgent problems unresolved. Interestingly enough, according to studies referred to by Levine and Rizvi, the areas of activities that give satisfaction to a person's life, "Evaluation of health, religious activities, and attitude towards government make less of contribution".[15] This is to say, unless people have reached a certain degree of identity with their country's past, present, future and a sense of responsible citizenship, political choice and political participation, is not such an important aspect of people's lives as some people have made it out to be.

Thus far, I have been discussing the dimension of freedom in the sense of emancipation from plight such as poverty. I shall now deal with the dimension of freedom in the sense of emancipation from constraints. Freedom is important to everyone, but sometimes the freedom of one may clash with the freedom of another. That clash becomes a constraint for another's freedom. For instance, in the economic sphere, we need a system to monitor the economic activities of people in free competition to prevent consumers being manipulated and exploited by the freedom of the suppliers or retailers; in the civic sphere, we need social and legal systems in which there are no unreasonable oppressive pressures on citizens by the freedom of the law enforcement community; in the social order sphere, we need a moral system for people's internal self-constraints and a legal system for external constraints so that immoral, unscrupulous, malicious, and criminal individuals could not exercise their freedom to harm the interests and lives of ordinary people and damage the social order. So, one's freedom always has to be balanced by the freedom of others and the social interests; collectively

---

[15] *Ibid*, p. 99.

considered, the social benefits. The question some would ask is what constitutes "social benefits". A discussion on this would easily take up another book. But it is important here to look at a few points relating to the urgent issues confronting developing countries we are dealing with.

First of all, some people are skeptical about the idea of rule by "social benefits" for fear that a government might use it as a blanket excuse to rule arbitrarily, like hiding a violation of individual rights under the name of social benefits. However, this very skepticism could be a blanket excuse of ignoring social benefit in the name of individual rights. I shall deal with this issue more in another context. Let us put aside this skepticism for the time being.

Second, even taking social benefits positively, sometimes the execution of them may be frustrated, not by any difference on defining social benefits, but by a structural problem of implementation in developing countries, such as the conflict of interests between existing social powers in a society. Indira Gandhi's headache about not being able to implement her rural reform policy at the grass-root level illustrated above is a case in point. No matter how good a policy is at high level government, it would tend to be derailed at the grass-root level, if there was not an effective organizational structure in place to implement the policy; especially in a large country like India or China.

Present-day China has similar headaches. For instance, even though the central government has been concerned for people's welfare in general, the political structure of China does not yet allow the central government to have effective control of the grass-root local governments. Thus, for instance, despite the central government's repeated warnings and closures of hundreds of dangerous mines, we still saw many serious mining accidents in China in 2005 and 2006. And despite the central government's repeated demands for wastewater control and the closure of hundreds of disqualified small factories, pollution of the major rivers in China there is still critically serious today. This is so because these sub-standard factories contribute substantially to the revenues of their local governments. Thus, there is a conflict of interest between the local government and the central government. Another example of the conflict of potential interests are that between the regional law courts and the country's highest court, because the former are under the local governments and not under the judiciary branch of the central government. Similarly, the Environmental Bureau is at the same level of authority as the provincial governments and not above them, so it has no authority to over-ride the decisions of the local governments. We see, for example in America, the district courts are directly responsible to the judiciary branch of the federal government (highest in America). Also, the Federal Aviation Authority (FAA), the Food and Drug Administration (FDA), and the Occupational Safety and Health Administration (OSHA) are all above the state (province) level in authority. Without going to the highest official in the central government to get consent, they have the power to penalize or close any factory or operation anywhere in America, if the factory or operation concerned does not abide by their rules and regulations (which are passed as legislations, and not something just conjured up arbitrarily by the agencies). It seems in order to solve the problems, all regulatory agencies should be on a higher level of authority than the local governments. And the local branches of those agencies should report directly to the central agencies, and not to the local government. And more importantly, they should get their budget from the central government and not local government. Otherwise, people tend to listen to whoever feeds them, leaving the problem of conflicting interests between the local and the central governments unsolved.

Actually, for a country to centralize those agencies, it does not have to raise the ranking of the officers working in those agencies (which could be a budgetary concern). The authority and power of the agencies should come from the designated roles of the agencies and not necessarily from the ranking of the officials in charge of those agencies. For example, when an ordinary soldier puts on the "Duty Officer" or "MP" armband, he has authority to challenge the misconduct of any officer of a higher ranking, during the hours he is on duty. By the same token, similar power can be conferred upon the regulatory agencies by the central government.

The issue discussed here calls attention to the fact that, even when it is quite clear what is beneficial to the society, there are political structural constraints in developing countries to prevent the implementation of social benefits. More and more of this has become an urgent problem in practical governance in developing countries. And there is an urgent need to re-think which part of the governmental power should be decentralized and which not; likewise in a market economy, which institution should be privatized and which not. Of course, this is always a delicate question. The rule of thumb seems to be that the operational functions of a government could be decentralized, but the regulatory functions of a government should be centralized.

Third, the emphasis on the important role of the government in executing programs for social benefits is not to opt for an authoritarian government. We have just seen how important it is to centralize certain functions of the government to regulate economic activities, not to speak of social and legal activities. For example, from the cases cited above we see that, if anything, the trouble with China is not that it is too centralized but rather in certain respects, not centralized enough. Freedom is important, and in order to balance the freedom of individuals with social benefits or that of a certain function of the society with social benefits, there have to be governing bodies to coordinate and regulate the activities. In China today, there is a centralized government, short of a universally elected one, but it indeed can work for the benefit of the general masses, providing social freedoms and stimulating the country's development, while maintaining its transparency and receptiveness by listening to public opinions. Actually, in this information age, it is difficult for a government not to be transparent and not to have dialogue with its people when there is the exposure of public media and the availability of popular internet commentaries. Some people always tend to use categories in political science textbooks to judge governments around the world; thinking that if a government is not democratic, it has to be despotic or oligarchic. If it is not a freely elected government, it has to be dictatorial or authoritarian. On 20 August 2005, an article by David Lague in the *International Herald Tribune* talked about how the media in "authoritarian China" were criticizing the government on public health problems, and went on to say that he was further surprised to have read that the government of China itself published a report on the shortcomings of the health-care system. Mr. Lague's frame of mind reminds me of my experience in China during the Cultural Revolution. According to the Chinese ideology of the time, people's ideas and sentiments were determined by their class background, it was unthinkable that we, coming from a bourgeois family background, could possibly be sympathetic to the "Great Proletarian Cultural Revolution". As a result, they concluded that the only conceivable reason for us (a family of five) coming to China at that time was that we had a clandestine mission. Although during the 9 years in China, we never suffered physical abuse, we were carefully watched. That was the same mentality as Mr. Lague. They had a preconceived idea of what we were, just as some people now have a preconceived ideological mind-set about China. During those days in China, not to cause further suspicion, I always kept our front door unlocked, and never had any cabinet or drawer in our flat locked, hoping that somebody would go into our flat while we were at work to satisfy their curiosity. So now, events have come 360 degrees around. China is keeping its doors open and even undesirable events "unlocked" on the media, so people could come and understand China. But somehow there are still people who tend to view China with an old pair of coloured glasses.

Of course, nowadays, everyone in China has seen the danger of having an exclusive all-pervasive ideology in a society, such as the the Cultural Revolution in China. There are many interpretations as to the "whys" and "what exactly happened" of that movement.[16] Having lived through 9 out of the 10 years of that period, my view is that since it was such a large-scale social movement with a major impact on Chinese history, despite its complexities, some people's

---

[16] See a general summary by Xu Youyu (徐友渔), "Western Studies on the Cultural Revolution" (西方对'文革'的研究) *Lectures at Beijing University* Vol. 4 (在北大听讲座 第四辑), pp. 142–160.

political ambitions, others' personal tragedies and entire social and economic misgivings, we must interpret it seriously, and not cynically or scornfully. If we interpret it simply as a movement to aggrandize Mao, or a malicious power struggle between Mao and Liu Shou-qi, we would not have learned anything from it. Admittedly, however we evaluate it; whether from the knowledge of social psychology or a rudimentary knowledge of social group-work theories, much of the unfortunate tragedies, like the well-known phenomenon of "private enmity settled on public account",[17] and the consequences of sending youth to the rural areas without organizational support, could all have easily been foreknown and prevented, or at least made not so catastrophic. But to analyze and evaluate the Cultural Revolution as such is not the purpose of this book. I only want to use it as an illustration of what we have been discussing; namely, the effects of promoting an exclusive and socially-pervasive intellectual/political purity.

To take the Cultural Revolution seriously at its most important motive, irrespective of what exactly happened and how it got derailed, I think Mao Ze Dong was indeed trying to pursue his ideal of a selfless human utopia, where equality would prevail everywhere. Some people interpret the Cultural Revolution as an episode of power struggle. Of course it was. Politics involve power struggles (in the best sense and not for one's selfish ends). For only with power in hand can one implement one's political ideals and socioeconomic policies. In that sense, even democratic elections are power struggles, though with a rationalized and legal system of procedures carried out peacefully and in an orderly way. If we read the post-1949 history of China leading up to the Cultural Revolution, we will see that the social programs Mao instituted prior to the Cultural Revolution such as "The Great Leap Forward" and the "commune system" in rural China, though unsuccessful and economically catastrophic as they were, showed that Mao was an idealist who seriously wanted to experiment with the ideals of eradicating selfishness and practicing general equality. In fact, Mao was very explicit that

---

[17] 私仇公报.

the reason for starting the Cultural Revolution was that he found that other leaders in the party were not interested in pursuing that goal, and was unable to implement that goal down the bureaucratic chain. This prompted what he called an innovative movement. "a revolution from the bottom up", a mass movement to challenge those in authority. What is relevant here is that during the Cultural Revolution, Mao's emphasis was on pursuing the sociopolitical ideal of selfless equality among all. At that time, Mao was following the Stalinist concept of Man, which was based on the assumption that human nature was malleable it could be changed. As David Munro said, according to that view, "All history is nothing but the continuous transformation of human nature".[18] So in the Cultural Revolution, Mao was trying to start a "revolution within one's soul" to change human nature. During that period, a central theme that we, as people in China, had to practice in thought and deed, were to "struggle against selfishness and criticize Revisionism".[19] People outside China with a mindset shaped somewhat by George Orwell's *1984* thought that China was indeed changing human nature; such as loving the state more than one's parents, and the love between comrades was more important than that between husband and wife, etc. But that was not what we found when my wife and I were placed in a factory to work after we first arrived in China. We worked and lived in the factory compound. What happened in everyday life there seemed to be the same as before in my childhood. In the southwestern part of China where the weather was mild, every day after work and supper in spring and summer, the workers and families would all sit outside in bamboo chairs with tea mugs on a stool beside them to cool off from the indoor heat. We sat around in different circles and chatted and told long tales, while the boys ran about playing hide-and-seek and the girls played rope skipping or other games. What we witnessed was that human nature did not change at all. The family was still the basic social unit. Family

---

[18] Donald J. Munro, *The Concept of Man in Contemporary China*, p. 11.

[19] 斗私批修 'Revisionism' referred to Khrushchev in the Soviet Union who had a policy, according to Mao, which deviated from the main spirit of orthodox Marxism.

members ate together and stayed under one roof. Husbands and wives quarreled over their differences, children fought over what each wanted to do differently, but they paid heed to their parents, and couples amended their differences in the old-fashioned way in bed.

When we moved to a university to teach English, we also witnessed that nobody was brainwashed. People exchanged their personal nonconforming views privately, but expressed the "correct" view tongue-in-cheek in discussion meetings about which even the political leader of the group slightly smiled amusingly. The interesting point was that in the entire experience we witnessed, there was no change in human nature. Self-interest was very much a part of everyone's important concerns, though the noble side of humanity was also there, such as dedication to a worthwhile cause like tree-planting and blood donation. Considered from this point of view, Mao's attempt to eradicate selfishness failed, but more important to our discussion is that the original intention of the Cultural Revolution to push for political doctrinal purity was undeniable, and the whole attempt was sociopolitically untenable. The result of the Cultural Revolution is, of course, history on which many books have been written: how the original intention got derailed; how the political ambitions and intrigues resulted in many people's personal tragedies; and the movement's catastrophic consequences in socioeconomic, cultural, and techno-scientific spheres in Chinese society are well known to all. The discussion here aims to show that to emphasize exclusive doctrinal purity in a whole society, people tend to be persecuted due to deviation from that doctrine, and important aspects of human well-being and enrichment, let alone the societal benefits, tend to be sacrificed. The demand for political purity during the Cultural Revolution in China is a concrete example. The phenomenon of religious persecutions due to religious doctrinal purity in Europe during the Middle Ages, and religious "witch-hunting" by the Puritans in early American history, are all examples. History has witnessed time and again that the glorification of "purity" breeds self-righteousness that always ends in senseless persecutions. What I have said here is not against wholehearted private beliefs (including religious beliefs) and wholehearted private practices *per se*, but is against an exclusive and all-pervasive system of beliefs used as an absolute requirement for the entire society.

Similarly, in economic development, an exclusive emphasis on chasing after GDP growth, might hurt the overall sustainable development of the society as a whole; such as the neglect of the pollution problems, ecological problems, and wastage problems, not to speak of the neglect of cultural problems. An exclusive economic emphasis on the "profit motive" in the market economy could also lead to a morally unbalanced development in the society. The market economy in its rudimentary form is built on self-interest working with the principle of supply and demand. If people in the developing countries do not realize that the market economy is only a skeleton, no matter how complex it is, needs to have positive social and moral values added, the consequence of the unconstrained economic force would only worsen the disparity between the rich and the poor. That is what happened in the early stage of China's adoption of the market economy. Many people thought that if self-interest was the basis of the market economy, why could they not be selfish and greedy. It is true that theoretically, if everybody took care of their own interest, then everyone's interest would be taken care of, as Adam Smith claimed in *The Wealth of Nations* (the "the invisible hand"). Incidentally, we should not forget that before writing that book, Adam Smith was the author of another book called *Theory of Moral Sentiments*. He was not insensitive to the good of the society. He just thought the "invisible hand" would support further "enlightened self-interest" and would enrich society. But unfortunately in reality, some people, due to their wealth, power, social influence, and even cunningness, could take care of their interest much better than others who were less endowed in those aspects. Therefore, the invisible hand of early capitalism as practiced in the West had to be supplemented by constraints of moral values, governmental legislations and, after the message of Marxism, the labor unions. For example, in America, the anti-trust law was passed to protect those corporations that were less able to take care of their interests than those financially powerful corporations which could monopolize the market. The National Labour Relation Board was formed to protect the laborers; the Agricultural Adjustment Administration was formed to protect the farmers; and the Social Security Administration was formed to protect the elderly. So, do not think that the American economy is still a laissez-faire, free-for-all economy. Of course, it is always a matter of debate as to how much the government should interfere with the workings of the market without damaging the contributive energy of the natural market force. The debate between "a big government" or "a small government" has been a constant debate of various administrations of Western countries.

In the initial stage of economic reform, the Chinese government also had to intervene in the workings of the market force for the sake of social benefits. At first, the government initiated and then had to ban powerful entities in the country, such as the armed forces and the government ministries, to participate in commerce. Then it had to ban individuals in the law enforcement community, or their family members, from participating in trades under the surveillance and check by the law enforcement community. China has learned from painful experience that aside from market force, the power-play in a society has to be recognized and balanced, and social or moral values have to be part of the market economy as guidelines.

The market economy could release people's energy and ingenuity to create wealth and stimulate economic growth. But it is like a wild horse that needs to be harnessed. Entrepreneurs in the West are now encouraged to be guided by moral values to counter such ideas as "greed is good", portrayed by Michael Douglas in the movie, "Wall Street", so that they should plough some of their wealth back to the society from which they have made their wealth. On top of that, a government also has programs promoting social benefits to counter the market economy's poverty-creating effects (in the de-humanizing sense). According to Barbara Harriss-White, the logic of maximizing profit and accumulation inherent in the capitalistic economy itself, if unregulated, will inevitably create poverty. For the raw market force will turn everything (including land, labor, and money) into commodities. The fate of labor as commodities with its possibility of being exploited, unemployed, and made redundant through costs saving or technological advancement are well known. The logic of maximizing profit and accumulation also creates wasteful commodities (toxic chemicals, nuclear waste, pesticide residues, etc.) that are harmful to human health, and harmful to the environment, by destroying the ecosystem through pollution.[20] It goes to show that aside from promoting moral values, there should also be dedicated economic programs like social insurance and public health insurance, together with governmental legislations to overcome "poverty", that is inherent in the logic of an unregulated market economy in order to promote social benefits. Capitalism, as practiced in America today, for instance, is no longer the capitalism of the 19th century. Many humanistic values have been added, though it is still biased toward maximizing individual profit and individual accumulation. It would be interesting to see how dynamic an economic system would be if the values of a "harmonious society" were added to a market economy as the pre-condition for maximizing profit and accumulation. It will be shown that we need to divide an economy into different aspects and then see how each performs what functions in order to take care of the social considerations. I shall come to that later.

The above discussion has indicated, most important of all, that any exclusive all-pervasive "ideology", be it political, religious or economic in a society suffocates the practice of freedom in development. Generally speaking, what Richard Flatham concludes is right:

> "societies and politics that are highly pluralistic and fluctuating internally, and cultures that welcome and celebrate abundant plurality and frequent competition and change, are most conducive to and supportive of the freedom of their members .... [it is most fearful of] human communities characterized by homogeneity, and more often than not, unthinking conformity. For them, such societies and certainly such politics are enemies not only of freedom but of the human spirit".[21] (brackets are Flatham's).

---

[20] See Barbara Harriss-White, "Poverty and Capitalism" in *Economic and Political Weekly*, April 1, 2006.

[21] Richard Flatham, *Freedom and Its Constraints*, p. 166.

Thus, freedom could be constrained, not only by political ideology, but also by economic ideology. Social benefits would, at times, constrain freedom, but it also need a free and open environment to be enriched. Coming back to the example of China today, it indeed does not yet have a universally elected government; but neither can it be said that it is an authoritarian society. It is moving toward an open society with relative transparency and pluralism in the governance of many facets of the society.[22] In fact, what used to be the propaganda mouthpiece of the government, the New China News Agency (NCNA) and the China Central Television Network (CCTV) have become the watchdogs of the government to expose irregularities and corruption around the country. If Mr Lague understood Chinese, he would have been even more surprised at what the Chinese media (including the Phoenix TV in Hong Kong) are reporting, and what political issues are being openly discussed nowadays. I think, at this stage of development in China, to have an open, yet centralized government is much more important than rushing into universal suffrage in election. In relation to an open society, Karl Popper says, "… if we wish to remain human, then there is only one way, the way into the open society. We must go into the unknown, the uncertain and insecure, using what reason we may have to plan as well as we can for both security and freedom".[23] This is exactly what China is doing today: trying new ideas and new methods, while holding on to some basic important values. When people observe China, they always tend to remember the doctrinal statements China made some time ago, or maybe they notice just the economic changes and not the sociopolitical and philosophical changes that China is undergoing. When China promotes an harmonious society today, it is not promoting a society in which everybody has to abide by the same "ideology". Even in ancient China, Confucius recognized that it was possible to have harmony with

---

[22] See Thomas Heberer, "China: No Democratization But Pluralization with Social and Political Implications" in *Democracy, Human Rights and Economic Development*, p. 57.

[23] Karl Popper, *The Open Society and its Enemies*, p. 201.

differences. Actually, he emphasized that "a gentleman strives for harmony despite differences, and the rogue is divisive despite similarities".[24] In music, the richness of harmony precisely presupposes differences in sounds, and yet they work in such a way that they could enrich the total coloring of those sounds.

Therefore, to emphasize social benefits in governing, the government might need to be centrally controlled, but need not be authoritarian. On the one hand, because of the humility, the pain and the social turmoil suffered over the past hundred some years, and the necessity for nation-building at this juncture of its history, China cannot afford to allow any social and political turmoil that might come from people's excessively free-wheeling political choices. Therefore, China today has to have a certain limitation on the freedom of political choice, but there are structured channels for political expressions through the representatives of the National Congress. More and more it has become less of a "rubber stamp" organization. And there is also the unstructured channel of the internet communications. On the other hand, and most important of all for our discussion, is that China as a developing country is placing priority on providing people with freedom from want; trying its best to raise the standard of living, the standard of education and health care (though there is still a great deal that has to be done); and giving people self-respect and dignity. At the same time, it has provided the legal environment in which people have the freedom of social choice. People now have the choice of what to buy, what to wear and eat, where to live, what to believe and worship, whom they love and marry, to where they travel, what to express in various artistic media, and in what to study and to do research. There seems to be a great degree of social freedom. And this seems to be the more important freedom at this juncture of development in Chinese history.

A point must be made on the freedom of worship in China. All types of religious worships seem to be allowed, but not if he/she challenges the authority of the state on civic matters. Even those

---

[24] 君子和而不同, 小人同而不和 Compare *Mencius* translated by Ezra Pund, p. 85.

countries that allow an authority higher than the state in one's personal life, never allow that on civic matters. The laws of the state have to be the highest authority. When there is civil disobedience, it could be expressed privately. And when it is expressed openly, it cannot be on a particular religious ground, but only on the grounds of a similar value that is also in the constitution of the country. For instance, I used to know a pacifist in America who refused to pay government tax as long as the country engaged in wars, but the condition was always that the tax money was in a bank account ready to be released if and when the country disengaged itself from war. So, he remained a law-abiding citizen. Although Martin Luther King Jr. was a Christian minister, and the movement against racial discrimination he started was inspired by the Christian faith, but the theme of the movement was not on any Christian confessions, but on the principle of equality and civil liberty which were also values emphasized in the American Constitution that had the highest sovereignty over civic matters. That is what the separation of church and state is all about.

Concerning constraints of freedom on a personal level, we can use examples in economic activities of an entrepreneur. How much freedom he can have, and how much limitation he must have for the sake of social benefits. Since the market economy, in principle, is to give as much personal freedom as possible to encourage economic vitality, the freedom of entrepreneurs is very much at stake. One policy is that an entrepreneur is at liberty to do whatever he/she chooses, as long as the activity does not "harm" or "offend" others, and is not "immoral" (J. S. Mill's Utilitarian Principle). We see here that behind the constraints are values that have been added to the skeleton of market economy.

J. S. Mill's values imply a presupposition of individualism. For what the principle emphasized is slanted toward maximizing an individual's freedom. The constraints are all negative, in that they do not specify any positive impact on the community, but only that one should *not* be immoral or would *not* harm and offend others. Instead of entering a detailed discussion, let us see how different the result would be if a different set of values is added into the principle, such as what Alan Wertheimer has offered. His constraints of freedom are under the principles of "collective benefits", "justice", and "need".[25] When an entrepreneur does not maximize his/her profit unconditionally, but consider his workers' medical and welfare benefits as a necessary part of his cost, the constraint on his/her freedom is an example of "collective benefit". When an entrepreneur does not maximize his/her financial power unconditionally, refraining from monopolizing the market is an example of constraint due to "justice". And when a developer does not maximize his/her accumulation unconditionally by building affordable housing for the low-income people in the society, the constraint is on the principle of "needs". Of course, aside from our discussion on freedom, a society could also promote "collective benefit", "justice", and "need" through incentives of governmental taxation. What has been said here is that personal freedom cannot but have constraints, and the constraints presuppose values. An economic system, for example, also cannot but have social and moral values injected into its skeleton. Some controls have to come from government legislation and some from private individuals' own initiatives. Both will be grounded in ideals with cultural identity.

In the political sphere, personal freedom likewise has to be constrained for reasons of social benefits. For the government has to be concerned with social order, social benefits, and the requirements of which might clash with the demand of personal freedom, provided that we are not dealing with a tyrannical ruler. That issue will be dealt with in Chapter 5 under the topic of democracy. Take China as an example again, from all accounts, China is not yet a completely open society, but it is relatively open in terms of social freedom. Journalists from the West always think China has too much control over the media. Firstly, we should allow for a different treatment of problems at different junctures of a country's history. At this juncture of China's history, the solidarity and cohesiveness of the people seems to be more important for the development than self-expression,

---

[25] See the general discussion by Alan Wertheimer, "Liberty, Coercion, and the Limits of the State" in *Blackwell's Guide to Social and Political Philosophy*, pp. 38–59.

though there is plenty of that through the Internet and the discussions in the National Congress nowadays. Secondly, some Western developed countries seem to have forgotten that when they were developing, they also had social and political controls like the McCarthy period in America in the 1950s. Likewise, in economic policies, the developed countries now insist all underdeveloped, as well as developing countries, open up their domestic markets for free trade which has made smaller and weaker countries very vulnerable economically. And they seem to forget that, historically during their own development, those developed countries all had high tariffs to protect their national industry. And now, after they are developed, they do not want others to climb up the same ladder used by them in their development. This practice is well-documented by Chang Ha-Joon who describes it graphically as "kicking away the ladder" (a phrase coined by the 19th century German economist Friederick List, 1789–1846).[26]

Therefore, control or no control, the Chinese government, through open expression on the Internet, now has many ways to know the people's interests and needs as to work toward so their well-being and also for what is socially beneficial. Fortunately, this could be done more and more easily today. China is not short of problems. But at least in the information age, technological resources can give the government the means to listen to the voice of its people, apart from the structured channel of the People's Congress. And the governmental policies and programs today show that the government is aware of the problems, and is responding to them. Whereas before, the radio, TV, and newspaper were only a one-way communication carrying the government's voice, the communication now has turned interactive, though not instantaneously interactive. Thus, in answering the skeptics about ruling according to "social benefits", the above discussions show that a centralized government need not be authoritarian, nor need it be operating only for its own benefits. It could be a centralized effort to implement programs for social benefits in a pluralistic society with transparency and accountability.

---

[26] See Ha-Joon Chang, *Kicking Away the Ladder* especially pp. 1–12.

And it has been shown that balancing personal freedom with social benefits is a tenable and necessary consideration. The government and popular responses to the earthquake in Sichuan, China, on May 12, 2008 has fully demonstrated that.

Having dealt with the skeptics of the "rule by social benefits", we now need to have a closer look at the "social benefits" themselves. Here again, the utilitarian principle of providing the greatest happiness (or answering the most important interests and needs) of the greatest number of people is still a very viable and practical principle for social benefits. But probing deeper into this issue is where we will touch on one of the concerns of this book: namely, the cultural identity of a society. For we need to dig into our deep-seated and most cherished values in our society to find the criteria to evaluate what we consider as important social benefits, though to identify those cultural values is not the task of a few people or in a few books. It will be a societal project for many concerning people over a long period of time, perhaps even decades. Of course, there are physical and objective requirements of social benefits, like the strength and wealth of a nation, the standard of living as well as the standard of health and education of the people, the efficiency and effectiveness of the socioeconomic, political and legal systems, the vitality and creativity of the intellectual and cultural life, and the environmental conditions that allow sustainable development. But, ultimately, the authority of the systems in the eyes of the people, the cohesiveness and energy of the people plus the moral fiber of the society which the people take pride in, all come from that cultural identity.

Practically speaking, China seems to be adopting much from Western liberalism, such as the market economy including the financial and capital markets and the legal system. But concerning Western liberalism, we should be aware that even many scholars in the West today are noticing the importance of cultural identity of various groups, starting with sub-groups within a society. There is a disappointment and disillusionment with Western liberalism in its inability to solve satisfactorily the problems of democratic political life, and a need to acknowledge and deal with the various sub-groups, by race, ethnicity, gender and religion, within a pluralistic society that have their own identity of cultures, beliefs, and needs.[27] Therefore, the rise of the "politics of identity" which calls attention to the importance of shared beliefs, interests, and needs of special groups within a society. In discussing the identity of the sub-groups in a society, Michael Kenny quoting Dallmayr concurs somewhat with what I have said about the importance of cultural identity on an international level: "Liberal individualism fatefully neglects the deeper existential well-springs of cultural life forms. The facts are that cultural groups are defined not by extrinsic attributes but by a "sense of identity", that is, by shared practices and by shared historical experiences and agonies".[28] China's Minority Nationality Policies are precisely efforts in respecting the shared identities of those communities. My position, taken as whole, however, is not a blanket or total rejection of Western liberalism. The very fact that I have chosen the concepts often trumpeted by Western liberalism to head each chapter of this book shows that I feel those concepts are of nominal importance to contemporary modern society. It is just that I do not take them at face value, but see the need to dissect them and understand them in the context of each developing country's cultural identity and with reference to its historical condition.

Cultural identity does not lead to a narrow nationalism, nor to "autarchky" (political-cultural nationalism). For, it is not a political concept, but a psycho-dynamic concept. Nationalism calls for an affirmation: "My country, right or wrong", whereas cultural identity, through a people's choice, places a people in an intellectual and emotional framework within which they can commit and dedicate their time, energy, and passion to what they have identified, and can function confidently in history. For example, witnessing the whole process of development of China in the last almost 30 years, we see that a healthy development needs not only political stability, social and economic astuteness, and professional expertise, but also moral

---

[27] See Michael Kenny, *The Politics of Identity*, pp. 1–3.

[28] *Ibid*, p. 130. Reference is made to Dallmayr, F. 'Democracy and Multiculturalism' in S.Benhabib (ed.) *Democracy and Differences*, Princeton, NJ: Princeton Univ. Press, pp. 278–294.

and cultural enrichment, and the social responsibility of those who are leading the country. Where it has failed is when it has followed aimlessly some prevalent system while groping. And where it has been successful is when it has had policies derived from a dedicated identity with the country's past, and with reference to present and future. What China is doing today; in many ways, reflect the traditional belief in equality and the ideal of the grand harmony together with the Neo-Marxist indignation at inequality and compassion for the oppressed. Thus, we notice that China today gives special attentions to the weaker and often neglected sectors of the society, such as the work with the disabled, the education in remote mountainous regions (some with private individuals, international groups, or with UNESCO, and World Bank' financial assistance), the rights of the migrant workers and their children's education in the city, as well as those left behind in rural homes, though due to the enormity of the problem, much more work has to be done in all spheres and at all levels of the country to approximate the goal of a harmonious society. Nobody can say major problems of China have even begun to be solved, but we can surmise the values behind the policies and programs implemented. For 3 years, China has been attacking problems of the rural population (between 700 and 800 million) by removing its tax burden and introducing scientific planting. Now, starting with the 11th 5-year-plan, China is trying to deal with the rural problem structurally: the farmers' property rights, their economic foundation, their purchasing power, standard of living and engineering infrastructure. This is going to be another enormous project in scale to deal with the under-privileged. It seems, however, that China while not giving priority to individual freedom of political choice, is putting much efforts in providing social freedoms and solving the problems of freedom from want in the profound sense indicated earlier. I am not saying what China is doing today cannot be derived from other value systems. In fact, I can easily see similar things be done from the secular applications of many religious confessions. But each country would have to have its own cultural identity, and China's identity comes from its historical heritage, ancient and the more recent.

This chapter has dealt with sociopolitical freedoms, and also personal freedoms with their possibilities and constraints. Ultimately, the purpose of any development is to promote human progress in enhancing human well-being and to enrich the human spirit. The rights and human spirits of individual persons, according to Flatham, are "sources of energy and vitality necessary to action; especially action in the face of obstacles and danger".[29] But more and more people now realize that the rights and the sources of the human spirits have to be understood in relation to a group larger than themselves. Michael Kenny says it well: 'Individuals remain the sources and loci of moral and social agency, but the materials and resources through which they come to understand themselves and exercise their capacities are shaped, above all, by the groupings to which they belong".[30]

In conclusion, we see that freedom is something everyone yearns for. However, there are different types of freedoms, and in developing countries, "freedom from want" should take precedence over "freedom of choice". The former embraces not only the satisfaction of basic physical needs for subsistence, but also the needs of what is vital to the human spirit, like self-respect, cultural identity, and human dignity. Therefore, among the freedom of choices, freedom of social choice should take precedence over freedom of political choice in developing countries, as human well-being and social stability are much more important to the vitality and creativity of the people in developing their countries. Moreover, social freedom will also prepare people for a position that will eventually enable them to be sophisticated enough to choose their political leaders on the basis of cultural identity. Likewise, when we talk about social benefits as constraints to various forms of freedoms, human and cultural values are at the roots of them. The uniqueness of a particular people and the criteria of social benefits for that particular society are, then, all derived from the cultural identity of that society.

---

[29] Richard Flatham, *Freedom and Its Conditions*, p. 166.
[30] Michael Kenny, *The Politics of Idemtity*, p. 131.

Chapter

4

Equality and Respect for Differences

As the purpose of this book does not allow a detailed discussion of the various sociopolitical concepts, I am only sweeping through them to see how a certain understanding and emphasis of them may or may not contribute to development in parts of Asia. Logically, the concept of equality is an aspect of the concept of justice which should be discussed here. But this chapter will concentrate on only one aspect of justice, equality, as it is crucial for developing countries. A detailed discussion of specific aspects of justice in governance will involve detailed discussions on very complicated issues, though one aspect of it will be touched upon in Chapter 5 where I shall be dealing with the legitimacy of who should rule and how a ruler should be determined, i.e., based on John Locke's concern about people's liberty and social justice. But that is one aspect of justice that is not much of an issue when democracy is assumed. The simplistic view of equality is sameness for everyone. The complication comes in implementing equality when everyone is not born with the same physical or socioeconomic and political resources. For instance, some are born physically normal and some with disabilities; some with extreme power of intelligence and artistic talents while some with impairments; some are born into families of dire poverty, while some into families of exceptional wealth and social or political positions.[1] The same treatment would not have equal effects on them. On the contrary, different treatment for some might end up providing more equal opportunity for all. For example, giving scholarships, grants or loans to students from families of less means would equalize the opportunities, or "leveling the playing field". However, I suggest that a thorough discussion of equality and justice is more appropriate at the fine-tuning stage of development, and not at the stage I am considering in this book.

Here, on the basis of what prompted this study, I would just like to examine the most basic minimal requirements for equality in developing countries, or the factors in equality that are most likely to deter initial development in Asia. Following from what has been said in Chapters 1, 2, and 3 of this book, a critical understanding of equality in the early stage of development lies in an understanding of the concept of personhood; that is, the respect for an individual person together with his/her basic rights and longing for freedom and equality. Without this rudimentary assumption (whether God-given in the Lockean sense or natural state of humanity in the Confucian sense) of seeing every individual person as a free and significant member of humanity who has due entitlements, there will not even be any concern for equality. Furthermore, according to the concept of the individual discussed in Chapter 1, he/she may be a respectable, honorable, and responsible individual, but is, at the same time, inextricably bound with others in his/her immediate community and even in a wider community of the total humanity. Thus, concern for equality is not an imposed obligation on an individual, but the natural responsibility of one as a member of humanity.

As a rudimentary understanding of "equality" for the government, Ronald Dworkin describes it as an "equal distribution of resources", rather than an "equal distribution of welfare",[2] because different people have different native conditions requiring different

---

[1] See Elizabeth Anderson, *What is the Point of Equality*.
[2] *Sovereign Virtue*, p. 15.

amounts and kinds of welfare. Equal distribution of welfare would involve an insoluble problem of having equal concern for very complex unequal situations. This book's position is that in the early stages of development where the basic standard of living starts at a very low level, the minimum need for welfare among people would not be too different. Then equality could be defined as "equal distribution of welfare". At a more sophisticated level, however, "equal distribution of resources" would be an appropriate definition of equality. What is significant in Dworkin's ideas, though, is that he says "equality cannot even be defined except by assuming liberty in place".[3] Here, as mentioned in the last chapter, the tendency of liberalism is to group all forms of freedoms under the rubric of political freedom, namely liberty. I think what Dworkin should have said is that we cannot define equality without assuming freedom, social, as well as political. That is, to talk about equality is to go back to the fundamental human demand for freedom stemming from the basic worth of the individual person.

From another point of view, equality is an aspect of justice. And to define justice simply as fairness, as John Rawls does,[4] cannot help us much. For while the meaning of "fairness" might be intuitively clear to the Anglo-American people because of their tradition, it may not do much to clarify the concept of equality. So Rawls's theory of justice is based upon a contract theory in which people in the "original state" decided to form an association by agreeing to abide by certain rules and principles, and the principles of justice and equality were among them. In this way, Rawls assumes justice and equality as a starting point, and avoids defining them. His attempt was to avoid going back to the Cartesian First Principle, Aquinas' natural law, or Mill's utilitarianism, though in the end, Rawls still has to say that "the most important good is self-respect".[5] That is, going back to a very basic idea of humanness. In either case, whether Rawls or Dworkin, the starting point of any discussion

---

[3] *Ibid*, p. 182.
[4] *A Theory of Justice*, p. 11f.
[5] *Ibid*, p. 440.

on equality is the basic existential human situation. And that is where I want to start.

What has been just said are the fundamentals of equality that I want to emphasize, because everyone is endowed with the immediate sense of self-worth which is understood existentially, and we do not have to justify it further. And through the insight of reciprocity, we can empathize with others having the same self-respect, same sense of human worth, and a same demand for freedom. That insight will give us the basis for our understanding of equality. While the Christian precept, "Love your neighbor as yourself" is a moral commandment, the Confucian precept, "Do not do to others what you would not like others do to you",[6] aside from being a moral precept, is also an illumination of reciprocity that is possible in human insight. This starting point is important for our discussion, because it affirms that the understanding of equality is natural to all human beings. And the most rudimentary goal of development is, after all, to raise the quality (in all ramifications of that word) of people's lives in a society. Therefore, equality should be one of the most important value-concerns of any government in instituting socioeconomic, political, and legal systems. Without respecting the belief that general masses hold equal status and have equal human desires and demands as the privileged officials of the government, there will not be the compassion to eliminate poverty and miseries among the people, nor the motivation to implement programs in establishing human rights and providing freedom from want. And it is the moral charge of reciprocity in relation to one's own desire for self-respect and demand for freedom that should awake the sense of equality which leads to compassion for others who may be very different from oneself in wealth, status, and many other ways. For example, as mentioned in Chapter 1, the concept of equality was realized in the Chinese tradition through the examination system that facilitated the vertical social mobility of anybody, including people of very low means, to officialdom and even to the position of premiership of the country. That person had gained respect, but at

---

[6] '己所勿欲，勿施于人, Compare with *Mencius*, translated by Ezra Pound, p. 31.

the same time due to the Chinese concept of personhood, he also had a responsibility toward the family, the community, and the country; a responsibility that was not an external constraint, but a part of his being an individual person.

Of course, the government's implementation of equality will require very astute consideration of many complicated issues. What I am more concerned with at this point is the acceptance of, and the attitude towards, equality by the leaders of developing countries in the early stages of development. Readers may remember what prompted the writing of this book was my puzzlement over how some countries in Asia that have adopted Western democracy which supposedly embodies the concept of equality, have not instilled the principle of equality in the hearts and minds of the leaders to eliminate poverty and miseries in their countries after decades of democratic governing.

I shall discuss in detail about the Philippines and India in this and the next chapter, each dealing from different perspectives of the countries. The Philippines, India, and Russia all have wonderful people and rich cultural traditions, especially India, whose Buddhism, though not a main stream religion in India, has made a major impact on Chinese and other Southeastern countries. And yet, it is a puzzle that after so many years of living with the democratic system that is supposed to champion equality, equality has not taken root.

In the Philippines, even those with university degrees could not enjoy a respectable living standard. It was estimated that there were about one million Filipino contract workers around the world seeking better living conditions in the early 1990s.[7] For instance, when we were living in Hongkong, just there alone there were about 63,000 Filipinos in the mid-1990s (about 1% of the Hongkong population); a lot of those working as domestic servants were university graduates. For that work they could get a guaranteed salary of more than HK$3000 per month, whereas at home they could only get a few hundred dollars as school teachers. According to a study by Yoshihara

---

[7] Yoshihara Kunio, *The Nation and the Economic Growth*, p. 225.

Kunio, well-educated people in the Philippines were frustrated and disillusioned, and opted to emigrate to other countries, mostly to the United States. In 1990, there were about 1.4 million Filipinos living in the United States, many of them professionals (doctors, engineers, business executives, accountants, and professors), and according to Kunio, they did not seem interested in building their country. For, in the first 8 months of 1992, their remittance back to the Philippines was only $10 million out of a total homeward remittance of $1.6 billion from contract workers abroad.[8]

According to the Asian Development Bank, the Philippines are not lacking in good policies and reform initiatives, but have problems in implementation. The bank summarized: "The failure in implementation has been attributed to many factors, including the lack of political will, heavy partisan politics, inadequate financial resources, graft, and corruption".[9] Aside from the financial inadequacy and the problems in social structure and officials' moral character, the first two factors in the bank's analysis are related to the government's indifference to the plight of the masses. The lack of political will and the partisan bickering are symptomatic of a government's preoccupation with its own internal interests and not with the welfare of its people. Although the Philippines has had democracy for a very long time and a relatively well-educated population, the government has somehow not been concerned enough with equality to eliminate poverty and raise the standard of living in their country. Kunio observes that there seemed to be a decay in moral values: "From the top to the bottom of the Philippine society, almost everyone seemed to be pursuing his personal objective with little regard to the social rules".[10] And he notices that "as the unscrupulous politicians gained more power, corruption spread in the bureaucracy. In the process, it lost the ideal and tradition of public service which had been nurtured during the American period".[11]

---

[8] See *Ibid*, p. 225.

[9] *Foreign Government Document* "The Philippines" 2005, p. xiii.

[10] Yoshihara Kunio, *The Nation and Economic Growth*, p. 229.

[11] *Ibid*, p. 217f.

The question is, what has 60 years of Western democracy done to instill the concept of equality? I shall deal with the complicated story of the Philippines further in the next chapter. Here, I only want to point out the facts of history that there is not a necessary connection between the people having the rights of political choice and having the rights of equality.

The situation in India is likewise difficult. According to an Indian journalist, R.G. Krishna, those in the government, before Dr. Manmohan Singh became the prime minister, were more concerned with their political fortune than with the poverty, hunger, ill health, and illiteracy of the general masses.[12] And according to another writer, it was as if, up to 2002, the poorest people in the world were all concentrated in India.[13] Again, the problem here is that those privileged representatives in the congress are like people in an exclusive club who enjoy their debates, but do not seem to see the general masses as a part of humanity like themselves. Of course, India has a most difficult social system, the caste system, to accommodate the concept of equality, even though there were born untouchables like Dr. B. R. Ambedkar who fought for the emancipation of the untouchables. And on top of that there is the complication of many religions and languages in India. Nevertheless, the same question arises: What has almost 60 years of democracy done to improve the situation? The answer will indicate that it is certainly a very involved situation with a complicated and complex society. I shall go into it more in the next chapter. Here, it seems clear again that the political institutions are such that they are unable to cope with the dynamics of the complication and complexity. One author summarizes the situation in the following way: "A relatively weak bureaucracy coupled with widespread corruption; especially at the state and local level, also challenge the country's ability to govern efficiently and to improve its citizens' standard of living".[14]

---

[12] R. Gopal Krishna, *India, A Nation in Turmoil*, p. 435.

[13] Stephen C. Cohen, *India: Emerging Power*, p. 2.

[14] Ganuly and DeVotte (eds.), *Understanding Contemporary India*, p. 3.

Corruption is symptomatic of all developing countries, including China, in which the universal rule of law is not well-established and where there are tremendous disparities between officials' salaries and the wealth that business people display in a market economy. I say corruption is symptomatic of all emergent societies, but it all depends on how prevalent it is. In some countries, corruption is overwhelming, whereas in some, bribes are called "lubricants" for getting things done. In order not to be obviously detected and exposed, this kind of corruption does not alter the quality of work and the economic target those officials are suppose to meet. They are, nevertheless, a leakage of the country's financial resources and a cause of unfair practices in business dealings and, most importantly, resentment of the government by the general populace.

Corruption in developing countries is indeed a terrible problem of wastage and root of tension between the citizens and their government. It is not only a moral problem, but more realistically, a socio-economic structural problem. Actually, large scandals of corruption are easier to tackle if the governing body puts its mind and courage to it. For using the accounting principle of "expenditure fitting income", abnormality can easily be exposed. There were cases in America where the "Godfathers" of Mafia groups were so well-protected by their hired lawyers from famous law schools that the government just could not indict them on legal grounds. But they were finally caught on charges of evasion of tax payments on their enormous wealth. Thus, certain types of corruption can be stopped through an independent auditing agency with the moral conviction and legal power to expose corruption, and bring the violators to justice. It is the "lubricant" leakage of public money that is more difficult to detect.

Corruption is such an important issue for inequality that I would like to say a few more words. For the independent auditing agency, the critical words are "independent" and "moral conviction". But I would add that the agents working in this organization have to be well-paid so that they would not be tempted. The economic factor joining the moral and legal factors in setting up the agency is important. For instance, the Hongkong experience has shown that if the terms and benefits of employment provided to the auditors and agents are appropriate, and the penalty for colluding with corrupt officials is high, there is a limit to the human desire for wealth and they would also be the least tempted. The officials in government are checked by a three-prong system set up in such a way that the officials "would not want to be corrupt" morally, "do not need to be corrupt" financially, and "do not dare to be corrupt" legally.

The three-pronged system mentioned above can work as a check on corruption of all government officials. It stresses that there has to be economic incentives aside from moral persuasion and legal constraints. The traditional Chinese solutions to problems tend to rely on "human nobility" or legal severity. But here, it seems the Chinese Confucian way of moral persuasion and noble examples alone do not work, nor would the Chinese legalist's exclusive emphasis of impersonal legal threat alone works. Of course, it goes without saying that there should be moral education and legislation against corruption, and the penalty should be appropriate to the crime. But more than that, there is a need to provide government officials with a comfortable enough living, medical, and pension benefits, and most important of all, in the Chinese case, to provide financial insurance for their children's university education abroad, as Hongkong used to do. There, all civil servants above certain grades had different packages to send their children abroad for education. Each culture puts priority on different things. At least in the Chinese scene, the rural people would sell everything valuable they own, like cows or pigs, to send their children to universities. In the city, most ordinary people are quite easy on material things for themselves. But when it comes to the best education and future for their children, they would be willing to do anything. So, aside from the isolated multi-million-dollar graft cases which can easily be discovered by an impartial and effective auditing system, very often the reason of corruption in China is the financial preparation of their children's university education abroad that is absolutely beyond the means of an official's life time savings. That is why we cannot rely on human nobility alone to fight against corruption, because the corrupt officials might even feel that they are being most "noble" by sacrificing themselves for their children when they receive under-table money. Nonetheless, to provide packages that include education programs for certain levels of officials might mean a heavy outlay of national resources, they are probably not more than the "leakage" through corruption. It is a matter of trade-offs. Besides, the positive gain of trust from the citizens would be well worth the economic outlay. Relative to our discussion, this is one typical case of providing national resources unequally in order to create an environment in which equality of opportunity would not be jeopardized by corrupt officials. Moreover, this is another reason for giving priority to economic growth. With the resources accumulated, aside from solving problems of subsistence poverty, and problems in medical, education and social welfare, the government would have the means to provide this kind of programs to deal with social equality.

Parenthetically, in devising policies and laws to promote equality is, of course, much more complicated in practice. They are not just promoting "sameness for everyone", nor just sympathetic towards the less fortunate. For instance, granting rightful privileges to those having heavy responsibilities as mentioned above, and allowing certain profit and wealth accumulation for businessmen who have made investment and taken risks are all part of the considerations. We cannot say when there is an accident involving an automobile and a pedestrian, the moving vehicle is always in the wrong, and the pedestrian (the weaker one) is always in the right, even though he has violated the traffic regulation. Theoretically, there is a basic contradiction between freedom and equality. If we push for extreme individual freedom, those individual with power and wealth would hurt the opportunity for equality of others. And if we push for extreme equality, we would jeopardize some people's rightful freedom.

More to the problem of promoting equality, the elected officials in both India and the Philippines, however, have a different picture from the one just mentioned above. They generally have better financial resources than the average urban citizens. According to David Wurfel, among the 40 most influential people in the Philippines in 1970, there were only 12 businessmen not holding public offices. And of those holding public office, at least six had been men of great wealth before their public service.[15] In India before 1980, when there was a recommendation from one party to fill at least 27% of the public posts by OBC (other backward classes) candidates, all public offices were held by members of the higher castes which accounted for less than 20% of the population.[16] Those holding public office were social elites; all had a Western education, or at least a Western-style education. Could it be that one of the reasons for a lack of concern for equality among the ruling classes in both India and the Philippines lies in the fact that they most likely had a big dosage of misplaced Western individualism? And in this way, could it be possible that they have come to believe in, and enjoy the privilege of, the freedom and autonomy of the individual without a consciousness of social justice and the concept of fairness that are part of the under girding values of Western democracy? Could it be, then, that both countries share a case of an alien individualism working in the hearts and minds of those people like an uprooted plant in a hostile soil without the nutrition needed? And would what was fertile with much valuable traditions in the native soil be suitable for a different kind of plant? For example, in India, there were dynamic personalities like Mohandas Gandhi and Jawaharlal Nehru who have actually tried to grow plants that could flourish to the rich native soil. Unfortunately, that work seems to have gotten sidetracked. When Indira Gandhi tried to follow that tradition, she found that she had to be dictatorial in order to fight the other voices in the democratic environment.

As mentioned in an earlier chapter, there is a similar situation with individualism among young people in China today. They take to Western individualism with a vengeance. They thirst for the expression of the self without having a social conscience, either derived from the best of Western culture, or from the traditional Chinese concept of the individual discussed in Chapter 1 (That "baby" has been thrown out with the "bath water"). Thus, they have an uprooted individualism and a personal psyche without roots. The

---

[15] See David Wurfel, *Filipino Politics: Development and Decay*, p. 57.
[16] See Francine Frankel, *India's Political Economy*, p. 683.

Chinese government is now very much concerned with this problem, and is urgently trying to deal with it from many avenues. One is to encourage a fervent intellectual re-examination of the Chinese tradition; trying to separate the grain from the chaff, though there are those who have gone overboard by trying to reassert the prominence of Confucianism in its totality. What I am trying to say in this book is that, aside from the effort of re-examining the traditional cultural heritage, one needs also to dissect the prevalent concepts for modernity and try to understand the nuances of meanings in them, and to evaluate them in one's own cultural context, so that one does not accept versions of those concepts that have not been acclimated.

What is being discussed here is the aspect of equality that should be of concern to the government officials of developing countries. Then there are also inequalities that are structural, as Iris Young has pointed out. Although her initial study was mainly in relation to the US, we can generalize the "five faces" of oppression in a society she identifies to understand inequalities in other societies:

(1) *Exploitation*: For example, disadvantaged position of women, minority racial groups and migrant workers.
(2) *Marginalization*: Those expelled from useful participation in society, and thus potentially subject to severe material deprivation and even extermination. For example, old people, unemployed, and disabled.
(3) *Cultural imperialism*: The thinking, habits, symbols, and assumptions of the majority group and dominant class or those embedded in the institutions as norms for the less privileged in the society.
(4) *Violence*: For example, unprovoked attacks on the persons and properties of the helpless. For example, women and children in some families and people of lower class or caste.
(5) *Powerlessness*: For example, those who have little or no work autonomy and could exercise little creativity or judgment in their work. They could only take orders.[17]

---

[17] See Iris Young, *Justice and the Politics of Difference*, pp. 48–65.

To enhance the cohesiveness of different sectors of society for development, the government of developing countries should be sensitive to the structural inequalities mentioned here, and to implement programs so that everyone would participate in the endeavor of development. Where there is less social inequality, people would have fewer tensions and more positive energy for development. We could use an example given by Richard Wilkinson to illustrate the point. He calls attention to a case in the state of Kerala on the west coast of India near the tip of the Indian subcontinent. It has a population of 32 million, and has an economic base in fishing.

> "[It has] undergone distribution programs abolishing landlordism, and redistributing land to the peasants; it subsidizes rice for the poor; it has a high minimum wage, and — partly as a massive literary campaign started in 1989 with more than 350,000 volunteers — it has achieved over 90 percent literacy levels. Kerala is also matriarchal, and the status of women, on many measures, is higher than in any other Indian state. It has an outstandingly good level of life expectancy. With GNP of scarcely $1000 per person per year, in the late 1990s life expectancy for men or women in Kerala was nonetheless only three or four years less than the United States. Japanese life expectancy exceeded that in the United States by a greater margin".[18]

And according to Ashutosh Varshney, quoted by Wilkinson:

> "Aside from good health and smaller income differences, Kerala has many of the characteristics associated with high social capital.... It has the highest consumption of newspapers per head of population in India...a remarkable civic-ness, a great associational life.... some with membership running into thousands.... In addition, more progress has been made in Kerala in overcoming the scourge of 'untouchables' then in any other parts of India, and large Muslim, Christian and Hindu communities have lived side by side with comparatively little strife".[19]

Therefore, apart from the official and social aspects, there should also be citizens' active participation in promoting equality as a mark

---

[18] Richard Wilkinson, *The Impact of Inequality*, p. 231.
[19] *Ibid*, p. 232.

of a civil society. The important point that Dworkin also stresses is that equality in a democratic society, aside from resting on the principle of treating all citizens impartially, rests also on the principle that "the choice of life must be made by the person concerned".[20] What is being stressed here is that equality requires a proactive attitude in respecting others despite their differences. In fact, the idea of respecting differences is a corollary of the concept of equality. Only when we respect others despite of their differences in gender, culture, ethnicity, skin color, or economic, social, and political status as equals, can we then treat them as equals. An interesting concept that has emerged recently, according to Samuel Schaffler, is that promoting equality is not a special virtue of the government, but an important ideal of human relations. A society can have institutions that promote and protect equality, but equality is not something that can be legislated. The point, to him, is that equality is not primarily an issue of how a government should treat its citizens, but rather "what it is for people to relate to one another as equals".[21]

Of course, a government with legislative power is important. Lesley Jacobs thinks that, realistically, no society is one happy family, though ideally one wishes it to be. So, equality has to be gained through a process of competition in a market economy, provided areas such as healthcare and education are not in the realm of competition. He outlines three dimensions in the consideration of equality that he uses as regulatory principles. Let us look at the first and the third dimensions first. In the first dimension, where there is social unfairness due to the backgrounds of people, like discrimination in social habits or company policies against certain classes of people, certain racial groups, or women in employment, pay scale or human rights, this is where the government has to come in with legislative procedures to remedy the situation. In the third dimension where some people completely lose out in the competitive market, such as the long-term unemployed or the socially and economically

---

[20] *Sovereign Virtue*, p. 6.

[21] Samuel Schaffler, "Equality as the Virtue of Sovereign: A Reply to R. Dworkin" in *Philosophy and Public Affairs*, p. 204.

marginalized, the government also has to institute or encourage, for instance, social insurance to safe-guard the losers to remedy this kind of unfairness.[22] The temporarily unemployed are also losers who need to be assisted, because for an able body to be without a job is not only an economic matter, but according to Jacobs, is also a matter of a loss of self-esteem, protection of health, pension rights, and social networking.[23] Thus, in cases where there is structural unfairness, or unfairness resulting from the harsh reality of competition, the government has to step in to remedy the situation, by legislation in the former case, and by social safety nets in the latter case.

Now, with the second dimension of unfairness, where people come from unequal backgrounds, physically, economically or socially, it is the dimension where people's relations to each other will play a most important part, because it is concerned with the attitude one treats others' background. Jacobs' most insightful contribution in this discussion of equal opportunities is his emphasis that there are no natural inequalities, even though some are born with poverty, impairment or disability. He says "...that the belief in natural inequalities...is a myth.... All inequalities properly understood are social...the real genetic differences may be natural but the inequalities that are concern of the author are social in origin, not natural".[24] This is to say the inequalities that come from discrimination are from people's attitudes. When a boy from a menial background is not being allowed to take an examination or a job it is not because of the natural status of his birth, but because of some authority's attitude toward his status of birth. A talented deaf and dumb girl is not allowed to enter a dancing group, not because of her natural disability, but because of the authority's attitude toward her disability. There is a well-known case in China where the dancing dream and ability of a deaf and dumb girl was recognized by a coach who decided to work with her. As a result, she turns out to be a tremendously successful dancer and is able to lead a group of

---

[22] See Lesley Jacobs, *Pursuing Equal Opportunities*, pp. 7–83.
[23] See *Ibid*, p. 163.
[24] *Ibid*, pp. 50–55.

dancers to express themselves in a dance of the Thousand-Hand Buddha with their hands in unison without the capability of hearing the beat of the music. In fact, she will most likely perform at one of the ceremonies of the 2008 Olympic Games in Beijing.

Thus, it is not enough for the government to reform social structure reforms and implement policies on equality. The citizens themselves have to have the compassion for others and for equality. The most critical aspect of equality in multiracial, multi-ethnic, and multireligious developing countries is to have people respecting differences in order that there may be unity and not hostility, cooperation and not confrontation among groups within the country they live in, and among members of the international community to which their countries belong. This last requirement is more and more relevant in the age of globalization which I shall deal with momentarily.

If we consider others as equals at all, we will be sensitive to their needs. Everyone has needs to be respected and valued as a person with a need for self-esteem which according to the psychologist Thomas Scheff, quoted by Richard Wilkinson, the lack of it is "shorthand for … having low esteem, feeling foolish, stupid, ridiculous, inadequate, defective, incompetent, awkward, exposed, vulnerable, insecure and helpless".[25] Any one of these feelings would emerge when people in social situations are continually being "looked down upon, treated as insignificant, disrespectfully, being stigmatized and humiliated".[26] If we all approach others from our own feelings and demands, we can understand how others would respond in similar situations just indicated, as long as we respect their differences and consider our oneness with them in humanity. Very often, inequality arises when we do not consider those who are different in gender, physical fitness, social and economic status, race, or ethnicity as equals in humanity. Thus, basically, social inequality is a matter of attitude, though the differences might be a "given".

Some differences are the given ingredients in this world. No matter how united a society is, there are subgroups within a society

---

[25] Richard Wilkinson, *The Impact of Inequality*, p. 93.
[26] *Ibid*, p. 26.

that have their own subcultures, interests, and needs that embrace their sense of belonging. And internationally, globalization or no globalization, there are different races, cultures, and nations, each with their own identities. The call for equality is not to ignore differences, but to respect differences, and treat others as equals in spite of differences. In fact, the undergirding principle of the UN's Human Rights Declaration is a call for unity despite diversity. Evelyn Kallen summarizes it this way: "The principle of 'Unity in Diversity', recognizing and embracing the essential oneness of all humanity, while at the same time celebrating the uniqueness of each human being and each human group".[27]

For a developed country, Sweden could be a good example of a country's and people's effort in caring for equality and eliminating poverty in the world. It has one of the best welfare services in the world, and gives a large proportion of its GNP in aid.[28] For developing countries, Kerala could be a good example of combined efforts of the government and the people in building and enforcing communities with a prevalence of equality. Unfortunately, very often we see the values of equality and respect for differences being smothered by certain dogmas and religious outlooks. Historically, the longest wars were religious wars, like the Crusades in Europe that extended almost 200 years, starting from 1095 AD, and the Thirty Years War (1618–1648). The fight between the Catholics and Protestants in Northern Ireland has lasted more than 40 years in our memory. Today, the Islamic fanatic movement, in response to the hegemony of Western culture and insensitivity, if not handled well, may turn into a clash between the Islamic nations against the Christian nations, as already hinted by slogans. Religious wars and conflicts might have hidden economic reasons and ulterior political motives, but religious reasons always sound the most righteous. In reality, there may be differences in faith between religions, but essentially there should not be conflicts among them. Conflicts are usually caused by misguided declarations or ambitious actions by the

---

[27] Evelyn Kellen, *Social Inequality and Social Injustice*, p. 30.
[28] Richard Wilkinson, *The Impact of Inequality*, p. 311.

authorities of certain religious leaders, careless mismanagement of policies, and a lack of respect for differences by ordinary people of different faiths.

When foreign religions were introduced to developing countries, together with sociopolitical institutions from the West, they came into conflict with different outlooks on religious practices of local cultures in many developing countries. According to Joachim Wach, aside from having a set of doctrines, a cult (liturgical pattern, symbols and the ritual of worship) and normative moral behaviors that all religions have, there are different types of religious organization and forms of worship.[29] Ernst Troeltsch tells us that the type that came out of Europe and America was the institutional type that was more universal in outlook and desired to "cover the whole life of humanity", whereas the sectarian type that emphasized personal inward perfection tended to "renounce the idea of dominating the world", or tended to be "indifferent, tolerant or hostile towards the world".[30] When the institutional type of Christianity came to Asia, it clashed with what Wach called a "diversified" form of religious organization and worship that fused religious practices with the everyday lives of the believers (though this form of Christianity seems to have become a dominant scene in America today, but it is still zealously evangelical). For instance, in parts of Asia where Buddhism and Confucianism have a major influence, believers do not go to definite places of worship on a regular basis. Maybe they go to temples several times a year or visit ancestral graves once or twice a year. And they most likely would keep at home an ancestral altar or an altar symbolizing the mysteries of the origin of life which, according to Lee Yearley, is the essence of ancestral worship.[31] Similarly, Qian Mu also stresses that the essence of filial piety is to

---

[29] See *Sociology of Religion*, pp. 270–271.

[30] See *The Social Teaching of the Christian Churches*, Vol. I., p. 331.

[31] Filial piety is an outlook of awe on the origin of human existence. See Lee H. Yearley's discussion in "Virtues and Religious Virtues" in *Confucian Spirituality*, p. 48.

acknowledge a profoundly respect for the origin of life.[32] In these places, the religious lives are not organized by particular institutions, and the believers tend to be tolerant of other religions and religious practices.

Therefore, not all cultures view religion with an outlook of exclusivity and evangelical zeal. Sometimes, even Christianity and Islamism, which belong to the institutional type, take on a non-exclusive attitude in countries such as in Malaysia, where Hindus, Muslims, Christians, Buddhists, and Confucians live together peacefully, or in Kerala, India where Muslims, Christians, and Hindus live together peacefully. That is possible when the government has the appropriate policies and the people have the appropriate attitude. Actually, in America, people of all religious confessions used to live together peacefully without certain Christian groups showing a zeal for asserting dominance until recently.[33] For that matter, a tolerant outlook among various religious groups is quite prevalent in multiracial and multicultural settings in developed countries. But in the days of the last century, when those religions went abroad to developing countries, they became less tolerant of differences, as if they alone had the "truth".

We have seen that if history has taught us anything, it is that any kind of ideological fanaticism, be it political or religious, does not lead to effective development in any country. In today's global context, we have to take into account equality, in the sense of respecting differences, to overcome much of the exploitation, cultural imperialism, violence, marginalization and the hopelessness in parts of the world today.[34]

This brings us to what I have discussed in the last chapter about understanding what "freedom from want" is in development countries

---

[32] See also Gad C. Isay, "Qian Mu and the Modern Transformation of Filial Piety" in *Journal of Chinese Philosophy*, pp. 441–452.

[33] See "Church Meets State", by Mark Lilla in *New York Times* — May 15, 2005 on the recent development of Christianity in America.

[34] See Iris Young, *Justice and the Politics of Difference*, pp. 48–62.

namely, to be emancipated from a lack of cultural identity and national dignity. And that dignity should not come from pity or patronization, but from other countries' respect of its aspirations and its rightful place in the world community, despite its differentiating uniqueness. Therefore, domestically speaking, for developing countries, the mere legislation of equality would only be empty rules if they are promulgated without those in authority having a passion for equality and without the people themselves respecting differences among their fellow citizens. An awareness of cultural identity and national dignity would bring about cohesiveness of the people that can generate an esprit de corps and momentum for development. Internationally, the more advanced developing countries, after having gained confidence in their own cultural identity and national dignity, should also take on their rightful responsibility in the global community by respecting differences and honoring the aspirations of the less developed countries. Before, going further, let us look at some facts about equality, or inequality, in our globalized world today.

Today, the problem of domestic equality cannot be separated from the problem of international forces insinuating inequality. In the first place, we see that certain trends of globalization are not reversible. For instance, the ease of communication (the Internet, cell phone, global 24-hour media coverage, air travel, etc.), the need for international trade, and the ease of capital flow that the information age and global interconnectivity have brought about, should be advantageous to development. But unfortunately, as mentioned earlier, it has created multi-faceted insecurities among the underdeveloped and the weaker developing countries. More important for our discussion is that it has brought about more inequality to the smaller and weaker countries in the world. According to the United Nations Development Programme (UNDP) 1999 report, if we do not take advantage and better share the opportunities of globalization, the failure in global growth of the last decades will continue. Now, "more than 80 countries still have per capita income lower than they were a decade or more ago, while 40 countries have sustained average per capita income growth of more than 3 percent a year since 1990, 55 countries, mostly Sub-Saharan Africa and Eastern European and the Commonwealth of Independent States (CIS) have had declining per capita income".[35] The report continues to say that in countries like China, the disparity between the coastal regions and the interior is widening. Even inequality within developed countries such as Sweden, the UK and the US has increased since 1980, though according to Mary Dowell-Jones, the widening of inequality within developed countries indicated here does not really have a similar cause as those in underdeveloped and developing countries. She points out:

"At the heart of rising inequality [in developed countries] is a technology-induced skill up-grading of advanced economics. Inequality has risen because demand for higher skilled workers has grown faster than the growth in the supply of skilled workers over the last two decades, bidding up wages. Meanwhile, wages for the unskilled have stagnated as manufacturing workers have been replaced by new production technologies. The observed inequality results from the skilled growing richer, rather than the poor becoming absolute poorer".[36]

While this might be true of the situation in Western developed countries, the deepening of inequalities between the developed countries and the underdeveloped as well as the developing countries is, nevertheless, related directly to the recent trend of globalization. The UNDP 1999 report further indicates: "The income gap between the fifth of the world's people living in the richest countries and the fifth in the poorest was 74 to 1 in 1997, up from 60 to 1 in 1990 and 30 to 1 in 1960".[37] Thus, overall, Manual Castells summarizes:

"the ascent of informational, global capitalism is indeed characterized by simultaneous economic development and underdevelopment, social inclusion and social exclusion.... There is polarization in the distribution of wealth at the global level, differential evolution of intra-country income inequality, albeit with a predominantly upward trend toward

---

[35] *The Global Transformations Reader*, p. 424.

[36] Mary Dowell-Jones, *Contextualizing the International Covenant on Economic, Social-Cultural Rights*, p. 140.

[37] *The Global Transformations Reader*, p. 425.

increasing inequality, and substantial growth of poverty and misery in the world at large and in most — but not all — countries, both developed and developing…".[38]

In view of the global situation discussed here, there seems to be an even more urgent need for advanced countries, developed or developing, not only to implement policies of equality domestically, but also to hold the fort against the onslaught of international forces creating inequality. The reason that inequality has increased in recent decades is because the economic theory behind the recent globalization (neoliberalism) is stacked in favor of the wealthier and the more influential entities in the worldwide competition and worldwide power contest, whether the entities are nations or individuals. Consequently, the rich become richer and the poor become poorer. Mary Dowell-Jones observes that international organizations like WTO and financial institutions like the IMF and World Bank have more power over the nation–states in operation according to the rules stacked against the weaker and poorer countries. International capital now has the ability to exit almost instantaneously when investors' sentiments are undermined. Quoting S. Sassen, she says:

> "…they [international financial institutes] have taken on more of the powers historically associated with the nation-state than any other institution of the last decades. The result of this concentration of power, she argues, is that [c]entral banks and governments appear now to be increasingly concerned about pleasing the financial markets rather than setting goals for social and economic well-being".[39]

The situation in East Asia is similar. According to Chia Siou Yue, an East Asian country's

> "ability to reap the benefits from globalization depends on various factors, including its stage of development, economic competitiveness and institutional flexibility. Countries best suited are those characterized by openness

---

[38] Manuel Castells, "The Rise of the Fourth World" in *Ibid*, p. 437.

[39] Mary Dowell-Jones, *Contextualizing the International Covenant on Economic, Social-Cultural Rights*, p. 143.

to the outside world, but also able to balance economic growth with domestic policies and institutions to minimize any negative impacts on vulnerable groups and individuals".[40]

He observes further that those countries that have a weak banking system would be most vulnerable to outside financial forces, like the 1997 financial crisis in Asia. Thus, some people in Asia are extremely critical of the neoliberalism theory. With capricious capital markets and speculators, governments in this area lose part of their sovereignty. Also, they consider that the WTO is "maintaining an uneven playing field" with the rich countries pushing for more trade liberalization while, at the same time, imposing barriers against agricultural and labor-intensive products from the poorer countries (causing demonstration outside of WTO world conferences in Seattle and Hongkong). Chia continues that East Asian exports are often restricted by anti-dumping measures, plus health and environmental standards. Furthermore, the digital divide has reinforced the traditional income divide. Therefore, jobs and livelihood are increasingly at the mercy of global forces, contributing to the growing division between the "haves" and the "have-nots", not to speak of social disintegration through the onslaught of Western norms and values delivered by the Internet and mass media.[41] Therefore, a country's indignation toward inequality can no longer be limited to one's own country nowadays, because in the global situation, the 24-hour media are bringing the images and problems of different people ever closer. This, all the more requires us to be aware of our global neighbors, to be particularly sensitive to the differences in the subtleties of the mores and beliefs of people in various countries and cultures.

While respecting others' differences and appreciating the difficult road they are tracking, some solutions must be found in changing the rules of the game whereby the lesser developing countries

---

[40] Chia, Siow Yue. "East Asia" in *Globalization and Equality: Perspective from the Developing World*, p. 98.
[41] See *Ibid*, pp. 98–108.

could participate in mutually beneficial economic programs so they could stand on their own feet economically; especially for those countries exporting raw resources only and often only one kind of resource, like petroleum, sugar or coffee. And it behooves those more advanced societies, developed or developing, that are capable of influencing and managing international affairs to have the moral obligation to counter those insinuating forces toward inequality by assisting the less developed countries not only in aid, but also more importantly, in developing their local economy. By standing on their own feet, the less developed countries would naturally gain their sense of national dignity, which is a crucial part of freedom from want. I am happy to see what is being, said here is also being promoted through China's foreign policies, with an attempt to further the cause of creating a harmonious world. It is very clear during The China–Africa Summit Conference in Beijing 2006 that China is trying to introduce a new international political economic order. The Eight Points of Policies announced there include many preferential financial facilities available to underdeveloped and developing countries in Africa and also the commitment to build schools and hospitals that used to be done primarily by private organizations in developed countries. The main spirit, however, is instead of treating under developed countries as only bases for supplying raw materials to developed countries, China is trying to build up a new order whereby the trading not only benefits a small elite in those countries, but also benefits more of the general populace, such as granting zero custom tariff for 440 items of their export products coming to China, and assisting the building of plants and industries that could use their own resources for manufacturing products which again stimulate employment. All of these measures are much more significant than just giving aid. What China seems to be doing is adhering to the age-old Chinese simple wisdom: "Give someone a fish you feed him for a day. Teach him how to fish you feed him for a lifetime".

5

Democracy and the Democratic Process

Democracy is probably the most misinterpreted, misunderstood, and misused word. For instance, apart from defining democracy as a political process, see what "democratic" refers to in the following:

(1) "Our family is very democratic", meaning, in our family, between parents and children, we respect each other.
(2) "That mass rally marching peacefully around town indicated how democratic the society is", meaning, how free and open the society is.
(3) "The physical punishment that school teachers used on students in the old days was entirely not democratic", meaning, the teachers did not pay attention to human rights.
(4) "That society is very democratic, whether between the rich and the poor, the healthy and the disabled, or the powerful and the ordinary", meaning, the society upholds well the value of equality.

Words related to "democracy" have been used in so many confusing ways, because throughout history, democracy has embodied all the meanings listed above and maybe even more. Among those meanings, whether it is the respect for an individual person, human rights, freedom, or equality, there is a further need to analyze and clarify each and every one of them for the purpose of nation building of developing countries. That is the rationale for the first four chapters of this book. Culminating in this chapter, we shall see that democracy is a complicated concept, and we have to be astute in understanding it before implementation. In actuality, democracy as practiced in the West also varies widely in different democratic countries. Broadly speaking, the Anglo-American democracy is different from that of the European continent. Leaving the confusion aside for the time being, let us first examine the institution and the process of democracy.

The original meaning of democracy in Greek is "government by the people", especially the rule of the majority.[1] In this sense, democracy is important to all countries, because they treat and govern their people at the base of all stable governments. Democracy answers the most basic questions of political science, namely, "who should rule?", and "how is the ruler chosen?". Historically, all peasant rebellions or revolutions, whether it was Zapata in Mexico or peasant rebellions in China, started when the existing ruler was degenerate, ruthless, oppressive, and not taking care of the welfare of the people. So people rose against the ruler to restore their minimum requirement of livelihood. The ruler is then said to have lost his mandate, and rebellion would be justified. In the traditional Chinese concept, the emperor had the "Mandate of Heaven" to rule when he took care of the welfare of the people. In secular language, it means he had the "mandate of the people". Democracy is important because it realizes the fact that the rule of a particular government is legitimized, because ultimately, it fosters the welfare of the people. Then, logically, it should be the people who put the government into power.

But democracy has often been valued as an end in itself. We hear people say: "Although there may be corruptions or unfair practices in the democratic process leading to an imperfect election, at least a democracy has been instituted in that country". This is a

---

[1] From the Oxford Dictionary.

typical example of individualism playing havoc, placing the individuals' freedom of political choice and the assertion of an individual's political right as an end in itself, rather than taking democracy as a means to take care of the interests and needs of the people as a whole. We have seen earlier that without satisfying people's freedom from want and guaranteeing their basic human rights, we would probably not have the necessary conditions to practice democracy. It is easy enough to set up a process of election, publicizing the backgrounds of the candidates, encouraging their campaign speeches, and setting up ballot stations. But the fairness of the election requires a sophisticated legal and administrative system. And, more importantly, the evaluation of the sagacity of the candidates, not to speak of their personal integrity, social consciousness, and what they would do after having been elected, require far more sophistication of the citizens in assessing the candidates before election, and monitoring their performance after they are in office.

Looking at the 2000 election in America, for instance, we saw how complicated the settlement of the race between Al Gore and George W. Bush was, and how complex the political and legal systems were required to solve the problem. Most of the developing countries just do not have the mechanisms to take care of such problems if a similar situation occurred. When we study the history of democracy, we see that Western democracy and the democratic process grow to maturity through many hundreds of years of trial and error. Each country had their own mistakes and solutions to amend those mistakes. The democracy in America today, for example, is a product of a long process of development, and there are still criticisms and evaluations of the system now. We also have to remember that when America was born as a nation, the enlightened political environment was already in fervor in the continent of Europe. During the 17th and 18th centuries, France was the intellectual and spiritual leader of Europe. Friederich Heer reminds us that Francois-Marie Voltaire (1694–1778) at the time was defending the oppressed, appealing for tolerance and recalling that all were brothers. And seeing the decadence of the ruling powers, he cried out for freedom, fraternity, and humanity.[2] Voltaire was also impressed by the freedom of politics and economy in England, calling it the land of democracy. The founding fathers of America were certainly familiar with Voltaire and Jean-Jacques Rousseau (1772–1778) who, according to Heer, was even revered as a prophet and saint in France at the time of his formulation of the "people's democracy" and the "general will" in *The Social Contract*. They were certainly also familiar with the Magna Carta (1215) that laid the foundation for the parliamentarian government in England, the Bill of Rights (1689), the foundation of English constitutionalism, and the writings of John Locke such as *The Second Treatise of Government*. Heer continues that Montesquieu's book, *The Spirit of Laws,* also had a great influence, especially its suggestion of a division of powers among the executive, legislative, and judiciary branches of the government, a concept that the American government used. And Thomas Jefferson, who wrote the first draft of the Declaration of Independence, had spent many years in Paris and was much influenced by the spirit of the Enlightenment on continental Europe.[3]

Although the French Revolution (1789) took place after the American Revolution (1776), it can be said that America was a child of the European Enlightenment and was born into Western democracy. In this sense, it is quite unreasonable to expect developing countries in Asia to adopt American-style democracy in its exact form without seeing the necessity of injecting enlightened values of different indigenous cultures into the democratic process and allowing time for them to develop their own unique paradigm of democracy. Besides, even American democracy has gone through many stages of development, not to mention the difference between the Anglo-American and the European democracies.

According to Ralph Ketcham, the definitive character of American democracy in its initial stage, due to its cultural affinity with the writings of thinkers like John Locke, Adam Smith, Richard Price, James Burgh, and Joseph Priestley, emphasized individual

---

[2] See Friederich Heer, *An Intellectual History of Europe*, pp. 382–395.
[3] *Ibid*, p. 398f.

rights and self-rule. Then in the 19th century, under the influence of Darwinism, American democracy emphasized struggle, competition, and indeterminacy in response to the concept of "the survival of the fittest" in the theory of evolution. American democracy in this period, according to Ketcham, under the influence of such thinkers as Jeremy Bentham (1748–1832), J.S. Mill (1806–1873), and Herbert Spencer (1820–1903), began to be concerned with the needs of the people, instead of leaning toward high and universal principles. It began to emphasize the utilitarian principle of "the greatest good of the greatest number" and the policy of letting people express their thoughts and having them contested in the open. A corollary of that was the emphasis on using the results from the social sciences in trying to understand what people's interests were. Ketcham continues that toward the end of the 19th century, John Dewey (1859–1952), sensing that the dual pressure from industrial organization and Darwinism was challenging the basic philosophy of individualistic liberalism and individualistic empiricism, called for "social planning" of industry, finance, and even all aspects of human life. Dewey termed this as "vital and courageous democratic liberation", the most important aspect of which was education.

Ketcham summarizes further that, when the gigantic transportation, industrial, and financial trusts that grew from modern technology and business came on the scene in the 20th century, the American government had to respond appropriately to them; especially after the great depression of 1929, the government had to have a central bank (The Federal Reserve Bank) to monitor macroeconomic matters and to insure national bank loans. It also passed many laws to control the powers of the industrial and financial giants. The emphasis was not only on corporations, on groups, and on the interaction and competition among them, but also on restraining raw power. Although free competition was still prevalent, democracy then did not encourage the traditional kind of *laissez-faire* economy, nor follow the governmental ideal of "governing least". Ketcham notes that, after WWII, terms referring to the American government as "the Liberal Corporate State", "the Welfare State", "Social Democracy", or "New Liberalism" began to be heard. But by the

1960s, people found this liberalism was incapable of achieving justice or promoting any higher goals. Then, during the Vietnam War, according to Ketcham, the students were disillusioned about American democracy, and the "Students for a Democratic Society" (SDS) had a meeting in Port Huron from which came the "Port Huron Statement" (1962), which described the government's failures: It complained about "military investment in cold war creating a 'power elite' that had made a mockery of democracy". It pointed out that while "two thirds of mankind suffered from undernourishment, the rich reveled in 'superfluous abundance'. The young people felt that they were "caught in a democratic system apathetic and manipulated rather than 'of, by, and for the people'". They felt that the American democracy being practiced in the 1960s was a "grotesque betrayal of the hopes and promise of 1945". Toward the latter part of the 20th century and after the Cold War, Ketcham notices, however, that American democracy was revitalized through a long period of peaceful economic and technological development, first by Ronald Reagan's policies against "state-enlarging", in favor of "state-diminishing" and "market-enhancing",[4] and then by the administration of Bill Clinton who had policies emphasizing progressive social programs, small government, a balanced budget, and elimination of trillions of dollars of national debt. While riding on waves of technological innovation, Clinton maintained a growing economy for the longest stretch of time in recent American history. On the other hand, American democracy today tends to encourage a government to be like a broker, balancing the various interest parties, and implementing compromised policies without much idealism. According to Ezra Vogel, America has now lost its national purpose after the Cold War, and at the same time, has lost control of the special interest groups and the media. In foreign policy, Vogel urges America, instead of being swayed by special interest groups, to be more cooperative rather than confrontational.[5]

---

[4] For a more thorough discussion of the above, see Ralph Ketcham, *The Idea of Democracy in the Modern Era* esp., pp. 1–119.

[5] See Ezra Vogel (ed.), *Living with China: US and China Relations in the Twenty First Century*, pp. 17–43.

The above brief survey of the development of American democracy is to show, as an example, that even in one country, democracy has been shaped by the cultural milieu of different historical periods. The skeleton of the democratic process did not change, but the philosophic and economic emphasis differed from period to period. Those changes were within one culture and one civilization. We can imagine how different a democracy has to be, if set in the context of a different civilization with different unique cultural values. Actually this should not be a surprise, for even in the most sacred sphere of human life, religious language and symbols would be adjusted when immersed in a new culture. The same religion would manifest itself quite differently in different cultures. Eastern Orthodox Christianity differs from Western Christianity, and American Catholicism differs from European Catholicism. Zen Buddhism in Japan differs from Chan Buddhism in China, though they both belong to the same sect of Buddhism. It is no wonder people view the unilateral export of an American-style democracy as cultural imperialism.

Some say Western-style democracy should be promoted all over the world because democratic countries are peace-loving countries. But that is certainly not borne out historically. Democratic countries used to go around the world colonizing other lands, enslaving people, and looting their resources. And in more recent times, we have witnessed a democratic country, for reasons that have yet to be established according to the rhyme of international law, that invaded another sovereign state. So, while the idea of democracy might be peace-loving, the actions of a declared "democratic government" may not necessarily be peace-loving.

It has also been said that democracy has to be introduced to developing countries from outside, because their leaders, by themselves, would not institute a governing system that challenges their own authority. I believe people have that impression because they are deluded by the fallacious view of democracy, thinking it as an unchanging norm, a complete and undissectible package which can be applicable anywhere, and thinking that because it is so different from the traditional way of life in developing countries, it has to be forced upon them. But historically, democracy in the West grew naturally from inside without any external force. Beginning with the Greeks, democracy in the Athenian tradition had the council of 500 elected by lot, at first to set the agenda of the assembly, and then to adjudicate proposals to the assembly by the citizens.[6] Modern representative government was initiated by the famous document of the Magna Carta, which came into being from the demand on the king by the growing power of the barons in England.[7] And parliamentary government was pushed further by the growing influence of the mercantile population joining forces with the knights in demanding their representation in parliament.[8] While stimulations might have come from ideas and experiences through international trade, the whole political development of the processes and procedures of democracy grew naturally from within Europe.

On the contrary, where Asian countries adopted democracy wholeheartedly at face value from the West, the results have not been satisfactory. I have already mentioned that the Philippines, after almost 60 years of Western democracy, is still not as developed as a contemporary modern society should be. The people's standard of living is generally low. Of course, the story of any country is a complicated one. In the first place, the Philippines with 7000 islands under its jurisdiction is a challenging place to govern. Then there is an Islamic and Christian conflict. Due to American influence and language, English language used to be the main language. Tagalog, which is a popular language among masses later became a language for the majority. The diffierent language groups also result in conflicts. As David Wurfel summarized: "Political stability needs national identity ... with the Philippines' diversity of sub-cultures and languages, it is difficult to have national identity; especially with the Muslim and dominant Christian division".[9] Also, according to Wurfel, due to its

---

[6] James S. Fishkin, "Deliberative Democracy" in *The Blackwell Guide to Social Political Philosophy*, p. 222.

[7] Antony Alcock, *A Short History of Europe*, p. 86.

[8] *Ibid*, pp. 163–164.

[9] David Wurfel, *Filipino Politics*, p. 25.

colonial history, the Philippines never had a monarchical tradition from which a country could draw myths to substantiate the legitimacy of political authority. Legitimacy, then, had to come from charismatic leadership, cultural identity, contemporary values and ideology, or persistent effective government performance. The last one was most difficult to accomplish due to the dissenting power of the old elites, the influential wealthy group, and the corrupt officials in the bureaucracy. So, in the modern history of the Philippines, two charismatic personalities were able to pull the country together for a period of time after the Americans left. One was Ferdinand Marcos and the other was Corazon Aquino.[10] Marcos came to power at a time when the country's social and political systems were disintegrating, and he was a cohesive force. But, although he ruled for almost 20 years, his term of office was a period of decay rather than development. Among other reasons, according to Wurfel, corruption in the bureaucracy made his government ineffective. His program of New Society ran against the interests of the wealthy and influential old elite, undermined the patronage network on which he depended, and antagonized the powerful social institution, the Catholic Church.[11] But worst of all, his financial policy relied too much on foreign credit. In fact, according to Yoshihara Kunio, at the time of Marcos' departure, the country had a foreign debt of US$28 billion which was a catastrophic burden to those who came after him.[12]

Aquino, with the support of the Catholic Church, came up on the wave of "people power" against tanks, and created an overwhelming "democratic legitimacy in the eyes of the public". But she did not institutionalize her initial success; neither did she have a clear goal beyond a return to constitutionalism. On the contrary, she allowed corruption and military abuse of the populace, and worst of all, she could not control the misconduct of members of her own family.[13] Whatever happened in the last 6 decades, the fact was that

---

[10] *Ibid*, p. 37ff.

[11] *Ibid*, p. 337.

[12] See *The Nation and Economic Growth*, p. 129.

[13] See David Wurfel, *Filipino Politics*, p. 338.

the per capita GNP of Philippines was twice as high as Thailand in 1950, but in 1991, Thailand's per capita GNP became twice as much as that of the Philippines.[14] In the mid-1990s, there was still a hopeless prevalence of corruption from top to bottom in the whole society. As a result, there is now a great deal of disillusionment and disenchantment among the intellectuals that has led to a mass emigration of the well-educated, as mentioned in the last chapter. According to the 2005 World Bank data, in 2004, 30% of the population was still living under its own poverty line.[15] And the Asian Development Bank, commenting on the governing body of the Philippines, says that, aside from corruption and internal bickering, it just does not seem to have the political will to improve the poverty situation.[16] The reasons for all these developments need further serious study, but for the purpose of our discussion, we have witnessed the fact that democracy coming from outside did not flourish in the Philippines. It was not because it was not nurtured. There was quite a bit of American influence in terms of attitudes and values and there was the establishment of the constitution in 1935. And it was not because people were not politically conscious. There were large turnouts at elections. According to Wurfel, 77% of Filipinos knew the names of their congressmen in 1950. Nearly half could give the number of senators as provided in the constitution.[17] But somehow, Western democracy did not take root. The people might enjoy having a voice in choosing their leaders, but evidently the politicians seem to be interested only in being elected, and not in doing anything to build up their country. All the values in Western democracy, like equality, integrity, and justice seem to have faded away from the minds and hearts of the government officials. Maybe the Filipinos need to inject some deep-seated indigenous values, both Islamic and Christian, into the democratic political system

---

[14] See *The Nation and Economic Growth*, p. VII.
[15] *2005 World Development Indicators* Table 2. 5/Poverty.
[16] See The Philippines, *Foreign Government Documents* 2005, p. xiii.
[17] See *Filipino Politics*, p. 29.

to make it take root, so that the elected officials would find building the country into a contemporary modern state their business.

I have also mentioned in an earlier chapter about India, which is another mature democratic society of almost 60 years of age in Asia. Compared to the Philippines, India is even more complicated and complex. According to Ganguly and Devotta, in 2003 India had one billion in population, and its life expectancy grew from 55 in 1950 to 62 in 1999. This means a population hike, and it would raise the question of how to feed the people and provide for their sanitation and health.[18] India is also a multireligion and multilanguage land. But with the caste system, the plight of the untouchables and poverty, especially among women, the problems are even more challenging. The women of India, Ganguly and Devotta claim in 2003, live most of their lives at the world's lowest level of development, on a par with their counterparts in Sub-Saharan Africa. Nearly two-third of India's women can neither read nor write. More than 60% of the children under 5 are malnourished,[19] though women in some of the villages now have become organized and are more assertive about their rights. Ganguly and Devotta observe that politically, there is a conflict between the policy of tolerance promoted by Gandhi and the Hindu nationalist movement which is more exclusive, with the assertion of building India on the basis of the Hindu religion, including institutions like caste. There is also the conflict between centralism and regionalism.[20] On the brighter side, Ganguly and DeVotte see that India has a robust civil society with an organized associational life. But on the other hand, the associations usually reflect the narrow caste, ethnic, regional, and religious communal loyalties (including patriarchy, class domination, and other tyrannies) that are deeply imbedded in the civil society.[21] Therefore, with the above brief survey, we come to the same question: granted the tremendous challenging situation, why has democracy not been

---

[18] Ganguly and DeVotta, *Understanding Contemporary India*, p. 4.
[19] *Ibid*, p. 139.
[20] *Ibid*, p. 231.
[21] *Ibid*, p. 82.

able to overcome those obstacles and reduce poverty to raise the standard of living of the general masses in almost six decades? What we see instead, except for the thriving of the software industry since the late 1980s and the recent call-center business outsourced from America that has produced tremendous GDP growth, is that India is still listed by the World Bank as one of the low-income countries (per capita Gross National Income below US$875). And the figure shows that there are still 29% of the population living under its own stringent national poverty line in 2004.[22] Francine Frankel notices that, even though the success of IT technology and IT business in India have brought about tremendous economic growth from 1994 to 1997, averaging a growth rate of over 7% per year, the economic growth has petered out after that. As mentioned earlier, Frankel concludes the reason being that:

> India's economic structure remains typical of low income nations which are poor precisely because they have not been able to provide productive work for a growing labour force in agriculture .... The reality is that Information Technology can only be a thrust sector in accelerating overall growth of domestic economy.... The full consequence of the failure to implement agrarian reforms and associated programs for increasing rural employment and social services became more obvious during the 1990s when the surge was exhausted very quickly once the global economy slowed and pent-up demand of the relatively small consumer class concentrated in urban areas and towns was sated.[23]

It seems likely that the failure of the Indian government lies in its inability to deal with its rural problems, due to the diverse views and bickering among the elected officials, even though everyone seems to know that the root of the problem of poverty lies there. One illuminating remark by Ganguly and Devotta is: "Appreciating India's relationship to the land is crucial."[24] Indira Gandhi, the one-time prime minister, saw that, but her rural reform programs were distracted by all sorts of dissenting voices in the congress that led to

---

[22] *2005 World Development Indicators,* Table 2.5/Poverty.

[23] Francine Frankel, *India's Political Economy*, pp. 611–615.

[24] Ganguly and Devotta, *Understanding Contemporary India*, p. XV.

her taking all the powers into her own hand, and her dictatorial methods made her very unpopular, which finally led to her downfall. The fact still remains that the basic problem of India lies in the rural areas. According to Barbara Harriss-White, the 1991 census showed that fewer than 12% of the population lived in metropolitan cities. Over 74% were rural and 14% lived in towns with populations under 200,000, making the total 88%.[25] In her study of this 88%, she found in 1999 that the "informal economy" (neither part of the market economy nor registered, but in mobile exchange and production; some of it is the "black economy") represents 60% of the net domestic product.[26] Harriss-White has discovered that at least half of the informal economy is black. And its impact on the macroeconomy is serious, for there is "a nexus which politicians, officials, criminals, and businessmen and their (often poor and dependent) 'runners' and 'fixers' are bound together in a mutually protective embrace. These are, in fact, the real form of 'collectivism' that dominates much of the economy".[27] And she sees that the only solution is to have a strong public mandate for accountability of the public office, an enforcement on tax compliance, and a clamp-down on corruption and fraud.[28] But it seems that public mandate is hard to come by when there are so many different dissenting voices in the central government.

In 2004, Sonia Gandhi, who championed the welfare of the masses by personally traveling across the country to meet people at the grassroots, promised the "Agriculture First" policy and increased public spending on primary and secondary education, enabled the Congress party to be elected.[29] She then let the reputable economist, Dr Manmohan Singh, become prime minister to reform the economic system in order to meet the urgent needs of eradicating poverty, hunger, ill-health, and illiteracy. At this juncture of Indian history, it is an extremely important step. This is

---

[25] Barbara Harriss-White, *India Working*, p. 1.

[26] *Ibid*, p. 5.

[27] *Ibid*, p. 7.

[28] *Ibid*, pp. 246–247.

[29] Francine Frankel, *India's Political Economy*, p. 777.

precisely the thesis of this book: that at a certain stage of development, we have to be concerned more with human rights than
individual rights, to take care of freedom from want more urgently
than the freedom of political choice. Economic reform will facili-
tate the accumulation of resources to implement programs necessary for poverty reduction. And by raising the education standard
of the masses, industries can be developed and employment created in such a way that the consumption power of the society
itself can sustain a healthy economy. This means that economic
reform and development cannot be isolated from the efficient and
effective implementation of governmental policies and programs.
Democracy is an important institution in a contemporary modern
society, but the question is whether, at a certain stage of development, a more firmly controlled centralized government would be
more appropriate to deal with the multiplicity of loyalties of religion, language, and region, and to deal with gender relations and
the complex social systemic constraints like class and caste. And
now, in the present context of globalization, it seems all the more
necessary to have an effective and efficient government, for
today, a sovereign state has to deal not only with internal problems, but also with tremendously powerful external forces for
decentralization, deregulation and liberalization of the domestic
market, including the capital market, and foreign trade, all of
which expose the country to an unprecedented international
competition. Many countries have suffered under the policies of
the international financial institutions. For instance, Frankel notes
that the international banking community thinks that primary
debt should not be more than 1.6% of GDP, but India in
1999/2000 reached 4.2%. And also, India's interest on public
debt, in that period, exceeded the GDP growth rate which is
extremely dangerous for a country's economy.[30] We hope India,
with the new wave of economic reforms under Prime Minister
Singh, would fare better in solving its urgent problems of freedom
from want.

---

[30] *Ibid*, p. 601.

Russia is another recent example of a country that suffered from prioritizing political freedom and Western-style democracy. After Gorbachev's initiation, Yeltsin instituted democracy through which people could exercise their voices in politics, but those who had the power to express themselves in elections were not at all aware of what went on in sociopolitical and economic development. When people woke up from the euphoria, they found that the country, under the consultancy of foreign advisors, had liberalized its economy and financial institutions to such an extent that it was burdened with extensive foreign loans and foreign debts.[31] The burden led the country to an "economic meltdown" in 1998.[32] Russia, under the spell of Western individualism, thought individual rights and freedom of political choice were more important than anything else, and neglected the importance of freedom from want that involve political and social reforms and economic growth. According to Michael Burawoy, Russia in its transition from a planned economy to a market economy, never had an economic transformation of the means of production and social transformation to counter the commodification of labor, or political transformation required for the national consolidation of money economy.[33] What happened, according to Burawoy, was that after Gorbachev's slogan of "glasnost" and "perestroika",

> ...the state has been hijacked by the emergent financial — natural resource — media oligarchy who bank rolled the crucial 1996 Yeltsin election campaign in return for shares (at discounted rates) in the most profitable Russia enterprises. They...more or less dictated the policy of the executive branch of the government. In line with the financial oligarchy's speculative interest, the executive of the Russian state has pursued short term borrowing from Western banks and collaborated with the World Bank and IMF conditions for loans. Although the Duma is more firmly rooted in the national economy, it is too weak to counter the collusion between the relative powerful executive and financial oligarchy.[34]

---

[31] Michael Ellman, "Transitional Economics" in *Rethinking Development Economics*, pp. 191–193.

[32] *World Bank Summary by Countries*.

[33] See Michael Burawoy, *Transition Without Transformation*, pp. 6–33.

[34] *Ibid*, pp. 21–22.

In other words, Burawoy shows the disintegration of the Russian state party that was unable to control the country's economic affairs, including production, finance, and trade. There was a dynamic economy, but the activities were carried out at the expense of production. Trading, bartering, and banking were all done under the control of a shadow government ("mafia"), and not that of the effective state. Burawoy notices that the country seemed to have retreated into a more primitive form of economy domestically. Internationally, Russia

> hooked itself into the global economy, and became enmeshed in the organization of transnational flow of natural resources, finance and information. At the same time it became detached from the local economy, raiding it for immediate riches without concern for its reproduction, let alone expansion.[35]

Because the Russian state lost control of all that was happening, it did not have the required economic transformation to build a robust economy; neither did it have the incentive and power to enforce the required social values to counter situations of inequality and injustice during its period of transition. Worst of all, because the state did not have an economic growth to accumulate resources for itself to build a viable economy, the country did not have the ability to service the international loans. The economy collapsed. Mere political freedom of the people did not seem to bring economic growth, nor social progress or a healthy society. What happened to Russia toward the end of the 20th century is another example to demonstrate the fallacy of prioritizing people's political choice in developing countries.

The above examples show amply that not only is good governance important for reducing poverty, taking care of the people's welfare and instilling hope and dignity in developing countries; but they also show that economic development is more important than political reform for a developing country at a stage when it is trying to pull itself out from backwardness.

China, for instance, only after 20 some years of economic reform and having accumulated some financial resources, was in a more confident position to launch political reforms, such as redefining the ruling party as a governing party, which would necessarily change

---

[35] *Ibid*, p. 14.

from being an *avant-garde* revolutionary party, stressing only the purity of heart and sacrificial spirit to an additional stress on the utilitarian objective of minding the interests of the broadest general masses. Actually, the government's policy for the past few years on rural reforms in eliminating central government taxes, and allowing farmers to trade their grain harvest on the open market, along with the program of "Building New Countryside" started in 2006, were all for the purpose of providing the absolute majority of the Chinese population with not only more purchasing power for internal consumption, but also with more political and social rights. The political reform also led to policies such as absorbing private entrepreneurs into the party; the reforms of the National Congress to include more academics and professional representatives; the revision of the constitution to emphasize more protection of people's property rights, etc. I am not saying that these reforms have solved all existing political problems nationwide, but that only when a country has the financial resources to stabilize the economy and be able to provide for the welfare of the people, including the provision of social freedom and human and national dignity, can the government have the confidence to enter discussions on more novel social and political policies, and to entertain more controversial ideas in reforming social and political structures. That is why Thomas Heberer, while not characterizing the development of China as democratization, characterizes it by a process of growing pluralization. Commenting on China's rapid economic change, he says: "This is not only to be seen in the extraordinary economic growth and the doubling of the living standard of many Chinese during the last decades, but also in the high degree of regional, sectorial and social alteration…economic change also cause political and social modification".[36]

Most of the confusions about democracy stem from some people using 'democracy' interchangeably with 'democratic processes'. Actually the former stresses certain spirits and values, whereas the latter stresses the process that gives legitimacy to the chosen leader to practice those spitirs and values. I have, hitherto, taken pain to

---

[36] "China: No Democratization But Pluralization with Social and Political Implications" in *Democracy, Human Rights and Economic Development*, pp. 57–59.

show that, historically, the latter process does not necessarily lead to the practice of the former. Moreover, the spirits and values of democracy can, on the contrary, be implemented in practice without a particular style of democratic process in certain emerging societies, albeit they might not necessarily be able to sustain the separation in the long run. The importance of the democratic process, however, does not mean we should give priority to countries in their developments. Therefore, we have to understand what democracy and what democratic process really are. When we try to scrutinize the democratic process deeper, we see that the essential process of democracy in its bare skeleton has basically two aspects: one is to give people the right to choose their governing officials. Another more important aspect is to provide a system to check on the power of the elected officials by having a limited term of office (the length of the limited term can be contextually decided). This carries out the mandate of the people in a rational, systematic, legal and orderly way. Very often, people tend to stress the rights of political choice and overlook the important aspect of democracy that limits the power of the elected officials by limiting their term of office, such that they would not be re-elected if they do not perform according to the mandate. This is the bare skeleton structure of the democratic process. Aside from this, values have to be added to the skeleton of the democratic process (in the American government, the powers of the government are further checked by a separation of its executive, legislative, and judiciary branches).

When we look at the human situation, it is a real irony of history that two systems, one economic and one political, that have survived all tests of time, and have now established themselves in the world today as the most workable institutions to date, are based partially on a not-so-idealistic aspect of human nature. A market economy is based upon the motivational force of "selfish interest" in profit within the natural necessity of supply and demand, and democracy is based partially upon the concept of the "corruptibility of Man by power", such that there has to be mechanisms of checks and balances.

There have been many types of social idealistic thinking, from Confucius' to Plato's, to that of the religious sects in the Middle Ages in Europe, the utopian societies like Robert Owen's New Harmony Community (1824), to orthodox Marxism, that all had hoped to build economic and political systems based upon an idealistic nature of Man, but history has shown that none of them had worked out well. And the market economy and democracy can survive the test of history because they are based on a realistic view of Man, and not on an idealistic view of Man. Of course, there have been philosopher kings and benevolent emperors in history. It is just that to establish sustainable political and economic systems, we cannot afford to rely on human nobility. Different religions and philosophies have their own concepts of human nature, and they all recognize that the realistic human situation we have to live with is not ideal. Buddhism sees human existence as a cycle of suffering due to pain, misery, and the frustrations from desire and cravings, that one is to be emancipated from this vicious cycle.[37] Islam sees human existence as constantly under the influence of Satan to commit perversity.[38] Christianity sees the original innocent Man being estranged from God due to his disobedience in the Garden of Eden.[39] Platonism sees that the human soul could pass to the region of purity, eternity, and immortality, but is "dragged by the body into the region of the changeable, and she wanders and is confused; the world spins around her, and she is like a drunkard when she touches the change".[40] Confucianism, as illustrated by the neo-Confucian, philosopher, Wang Yangming (王陽明 1472–1529), stresses moral perfection lies in discovering one's innate goodness, but "that innate principle is constantly in danger of being obscured by rationalization and selfish desires".[41] Even Marx, in his early writings, talked about the industrial-age Man being alienated from his essential nature, his community, and his humanity.[42] All the above traditions see the realistic human

---

[37] See Langley Myrtle, *World Religion*, pp. 80–86.

[38] *Ibid*, pp. 327–339.

[39] *Ibid*, pp. 272–279.

[40] See Plato, *Phaedo*.

[41] See Langley Myrttle, *World Religion*, p. 125.

[42] *Early Writings of Karl Marx*, p. 429f.

situation as not what it ought to be, and yet recognize it as the inescapable human situation that we have to face in our existence.

But all these traditions do not say human nature is hopelessly depraved. There have been very wise and saintly figures in human history who rose above the fallen state and left the world noble ideas and values for perpetuity like the great sages and thinkers, and also those who could rise up at crucial moments to perform selfless and courageous acts for worthy causes, like revolutionary heroes and martyrs. These possibilities enable us to think about noble ideas and values, and live according to them. That is why the Buddhist tradition honors the white lotus flower that grows in a muddy pond, because the purity of the white flower could rise out of the black murky mud without being contaminated by the dirt. In the Christian tradition, the sinful Man could be forgiven and redeemed, and thereby be renewed to be joyful and useful to humanity. In the Confucian tradition, a person could be morally righteous, if he/she only listens to his/her inner conscience and is not side-tracked by selfishness. These examples show that, on occasions, human beings have the ability to be righteous and act morally, and could be compassionate toward fellow human beings, especially if there is a noble and worthy cause to be accomplished. This is another example of the both/and logic discussed in Chapter 1 in relation to human nature.

However, the successful staying power of the market economy and democracy indicates that, for a sustainable foundation of an economic system or a political institution, we hope to have noble people to rule the country, but at the same time, we cannot afford to rely on this human nobility, because the fallen state and frailty of human nature is susceptible to temptations; the temptation of selfishness and power being two of the most critical ones. Thus, we must devise systems through which we can check the selfish tendencies and the power centers, though, of course, we should also encourage, promote, and provide incentives for human nobility in socioeconomic and political endeavors. I shall deal more with the importance of legal check on powers in Chapter 6, but here we need only point out that in devising political or economic systems, we have to base their principles on a realistic view of Man and not on an idealistic view of Man. Otherwise, we shall forever be waiting for a wise and benevolent leader to appear. And even if he does appear, it would only be for the limited period of his lifetime. Actually, there were cases in Chinese history, like in early Tang Dynasty, where when a wise and benevolent emperor came on the scene, the lives of the people and culture flourished, and the society was politically stable and economically thriving, but those splendors only lasted as long as those emperors lasted.

For instance, the present government of China is very open and willing to listen to its "Think Tank", to the representatives in the People's Congress, the reports of the media, and people's views via the Internet. As a result, the government is considered by the Chinese people at large, as reasonable, flexible, caring for its people, and sagacious in nation-building. There might still be many problems to overcome, but at least the government is considered earnest in trying to solve them one by one and step by step. However, in the long run, we do not know who might happen to be the next leaders of the country. A mature and sustainable political system cannot change as leadership changes. Thus, in building that mature and sustainable system, our philosophic foundation cannot depend too heavily on the nobility of those who govern. Here is one instance where we have to part company with the Confucian ideal of "Rule by moral persuasion and personal example". Of course, neither should we jump to the other extreme — the legalist's "rule by impersonal law" alone. The political system has to be built on the basis of a realistic view of Man which says that a completely moral person may be tempted by selfishness and become corrupt when given power, and needs to be checked by another political mechanism. Therefore, democratic process is important not because it is something modern we must emulate, but because it confirms a lesson from historical reality. The nature of democracy in relation to human nature can best be described by Reinhold Niebuhr's dictum: "Man's capacity for justice makes democracy possible, but his inclination to injustice makes democracy necessary".[43]

---

[43] *The Children of Light and the Children of Darkness*, p. xi.

Recognizing the realistic human situation is the basis for establishing a solid foundation of a stable political system. However, recognizing the democratic process of popular election plus a mechanism to limit the power of the elected as only a rudimentary skeleton, we need to see that noble values have to be added into that skeleton to serve the interest, needs, and welfare of the people. Often, those who believe democracy as an end in itself are ecstatic when large crowds turn out to vote (who would not be excited when given the freedom to choose?), but they tend to forget that the right to vote is only half of what makes democracy important. The other half is what the elected officials will do after they are elected, and what they will do depends on the values they subscribe. I have chosen to analyze those concepts that head each chapter of this book, because they, among others, are crucial concepts informing good governance of a contemporary modern society after being analyzed and understood in cultural context. If we do not add positive values derived from such concepts into the skeleton, the consequences of the democratic process could be devastating. As in the examples cited above, we could see much fanfare at political campaigns, but not much action to alleviate the plight of their people after the candidates were elected. They could do that with good conscience because they thought the voting process alone by itself was good enough. Although Western democracy carries with it many positive values, they are never thought by the elected officials to be there in democracy. The irony is, even if they did notice values had to be added, they tended to add values derived from individualism which most likely do not speak to the situations in Asian countries.

Actually, as mentioned in Chapter 4, all developing countries have their own deep-seated and noble values to base their development on. The point being stressed here is that aside from analyzing the concept of democracy to see the democratic process as only a skeleton, it is necessary to see that a successful democracy must also carry social values with it. And in order for a democracy to work well in a particular country, it must include those indigenous values cherished by the people of that country. Ultimately, the end of any good political system is to have the elected officials working for the benefit of the people and the society, and not just merely to have mass rallies at political campaigns and a lot of fanfare at elections. Otherwise, it would only be "full of sound and fury signifying nothing". For instance, China is promoting a harmonious society, because as mentioned in the Introduction of this book, "the grand harmony" has been a time-honored ideal of the Chinese tradition. And China is also emphasizing equality which is another most cherished value in the Chinese heritage, as exemplified by the examination system. These values with cultural identity should naturally be a part of the important intellectual foundation of China's development.

The market economy has the same story as democracy. Actually, the desire and the accomplishment of accumulating wealth is as old as the history of trading. But modern capitalism in the West, according to Max Weber, was unique in that it was driven by a spirit that, unlike what drove the previous commercial aristocracy, could be traced to the 16th-century religious ethics of Calvinism that considered making money with ascetic hard work and frugality a calling in one's life. Weber further points out that, according to this spirit, "Man is dominated by the making of money and acquisition as the ultimate purpose of life".[44] Whereas the work ethics undergirding capitalism has somewhat faded today, it nevertheless shows that the economic system is not without any social values embedded in it. And we have witnessed that in the growth of capitalism in the West, many more social values have to be added to the legal system to protect the financially less powerful and the ordinary consumers. The raw power of entrepreneurship has to be checked by the laws based upon deep-seated and most cherished social values of a culture.

The above discussions indicate that development is a long process of socioeconomic and political reforms, interspersed with considerations and the implementation of suitable social, moral, and cultural values undergirding the legal system. Any hasty adoption of democracy without considering the added values, or worse yet,

---

[44] *The Protestant Ethic and the Spirit of Capitalism*, pp. 47–78.

without realizing that the democratic process or economic system needing indigenous social values to be added, could have been one of the important reasons why democracies have not been successful in building some Asian countries into contemporary modern states.

Moreover, the implementation of democracy, like other things, should follow the dictum: "There is a time and place for everything". If we were to use Abraham Lincoln's dictum on democracy in the Gettysburg Address — "government of the people, by the people and for the people", developing countries might realize democracy in a historical sequence of those phrases, but in a slightly different order. In the first place, a group of people who could become the ruling body, must have initially gained the support of the majority of the people, to have the mandate of the people. For instance, in pre-1949 China, it would be unthinkable that the ill-equipped revolutionary army of the Chinese Communist Party, could fight the much better equipped Japanese army in parts of China and the even better American-equipped KMT army later, had they not had the support of the general populace. The secret was that wherever they went, they redistributed land to the poor peasants as well as maintained the strict discipline of what the revolutionary army called the "Three Main Rules of Disciplines and Eight Points for Attention",[45] which

---

[45] *The Selected Works of Mao Tse-Tung* Vol. IV, p. 155.

The Three Main Rules of Disciplines are:

   (1) Obey order in all your actions.
   (2) Do not take a single needle or piece of thread from the masses.
   (3) Turn in everything captured.

The Eight Points for Attention are:.

   (1) Speak politely.
   (2) Pay fairly for what you buy.
   (3) Return everything you borrow.
   (4) Pay for everything you damage.
   (5) Do not hit or swear at people.
   (6) Do not damage crops.
   (7) Do not take liberties with women.
   (8) Do not ill-treat captives.

were very commonsensical rulings, but effective in winning the hearts of people. For example, it strictly forbade the common military practices in those days of looting and raping in each village an army entered, and it strictly respected the properties of the people. They could overcome extreme difficulties and be victorious, because the whole population in the countryside and intellectuals in the cities were behind them. So, at that stage, the government was a *government of the people.*

In the previous chapters when I talked about human rights, freedom, and equality, I said that, for the time being, those discussions assumed the country was not ruled by tyrants. Now we have to ask the questions: How could tyrants come to take care of their people in those areas? If they do not, what can the people do about them? In the first place, we see that in order to become the ruler of the people, even tyrants have to do something or promise something that would be welcomed by the people, to show that they are rulers *of the people.* Secondly, if they are ruthless and oppressive after becoming the rulers, they cannot be considered a government of the people. Then, soon beyond a tolerable point, people would rise up against them. Historically, that was how peasant rebellions, military coup etats, and revolutions started. And some were successful and good for the people and some were failures or turned out to be even worse than before, depending on whether the revolting group had a culturally identifiable ideal and political platform and workable strategy. In the past, the basic legitimacy of revolt was from the concept of "the Mandate of Heaven" in China, and now in secular language, that would be called "the Mandate of the People".

The crucial question for our discussion is: What if a tyrant is so oppressive and ruthless in his means of controlling the dissenting voices that the people do not have a chance to stage a successful revolt? It seems that there were no other ways other than those just mentioned to overthrow the tyrants. But now there seems to be a theory that says "some external force has a moral duty to save those suffering people from the tyrants, if the people could not do that themselves internally; namely human rights are more important than sovereignty rights". This has made the picture much more complicated, because the justification and effectiveness of the acts of the external force depend greatly upon how well the external force understands the local situation, its mores, taboos, religions, various subcultures, and the essence of the sociopolitical problems. Fortunately today, we have the United Nations which has the legitimacy to go into that country to have a thorough and relatively objective understanding of the situation and a relatively representative consensus for action. Thus, today, a solution to check the tyranny within a country could come from the organization of the United Nations. However, if the external force bypass the United Nations and goes into a country without a thorough understanding of the situation, first of all, it violates the international law of one sovereign nation invading another sovereign nation without justification. And secondly, if the external force, for "undeclared reasons" and without a thorough understanding of the complexity of the situation, goes into this unknown territory, it would be like opening up the lid of a black box leading to a prolific source of troubles. The present situation in Iraq is just a case in point. There are various studies and interpretations of the total violent civilian deaths in Iraq since the invasion. But the known results are already devastating. It is true that the tyrant has been removed for good, but what is the justification for the violent deaths of 655,000[46] innocent Iraqis in 2006 and with that number increasing everyday by tens or even hundreds? And what is the justification for turning millions of people of the second richest country in the Middle East into refugees and displaced persons in foreign lands? Is that huge human cost, constant terror over the loss of personal security, grieving of the lost of loved ones and the hopelessness of homelessness better than the conditions under the tyrant? Only history can make a judgment on that.

---

[46] Figure given by *The Guardian* (October 11, 2006) according to a study by the British medical journal, *Lancet*.

Therefore, after a group has established a government of the people, it has to do things for the welfare and benefit of the broad spectrum of people in that country to maintain the mandate of the people. In China's case, for example, Mao Zedong was very conscious who gave the Chinese Communist Party (CCP) the power to rule, and was very specific about the mandate. At one point he stressed:

> Another hallmark distinguishing our Party from all other political parties is that we have very close ties with the broadest masses of the people. Our point of departure is to serve the people wholeheartedly, and never for a moment divorce ourselves from the masses, to proceed in all cases from the interests of the people, and not from the interests of individuals or groups.... It [the Party] should teach every comrade to love the people and listen attentively to the voice of the masses; to identity himself with the masses wherever he goes, instead of standing above them. [He] should immerse himself among them....[47]

In other words, the government has to provide the people with freedom from want, to implement programs to realize people's human rights, to build up not only economic and engineering infrastructures, but also social political infrastructure to guarantee cultural flourishing plus law and order in a society, and most important of all, to act in such a way that it gives dignity and hope to the people. Implementations usually involve a tremendous amount of practical difficulties and hard work. It is in these areas of work that cultural identity becomes very important, for in making decisions for each item of work, aside from technical and professional expertise, they are always set in a framework of macroplanning which has to be informed by social ideals and values that are beneficial to the society and the people, and accepted by people as significant and important. At this stage, the government can reasonably be called a *government for the people*. And according to the amount and complexity of the problems in development, this could be a long period.

---

[47] *The Selected Works of Mao Tse-Tung* Vol. III, p. 315.

Aside from technoscientific, socioeconomic, and legal progress with which the majority of people have been emancipated from the preoccupation of their livelihood, gaining their freedom from want, and their social freedom, the people would then feel that they have the responsibility to participate in the overall growth and development of the society. That is, beside taking part in the building of the country in the socioeconomic and legal aspects, they would want to have a voice in the political process of evaluating policies, deciding on legislation, and choosing and monitoring governing officials. On the part of the governmental officials, through decades of successful development in this direction, they would have the confidence to naturally consider themselves as members of the total population performing certain special functions in a society, and not a special group juxtapose against the population. As indeed, historically, all officials in China rose from the general populace. It is even more so in the long-standing tradition of the present Party in China. The important thing in a mature and stable political environment is that the democratic process of election and term of office would remind the officials of who put them in power. Of course, there will always be political parties and party disciplines, but they will be parties grown out of responsible concerns of some to serve the people and not a special entity sitting on top of the people. When a system of political institution is established on such a basis, then we have a *government by the people.* Historically, the process could go in the reverse direction. When leaders of some countries thought they had already got the ultimate in political life, and that there was no reason to further improve the welfare of the society, they do not become a government for the people, even though they started out as one. If this deterioration goes on, people would gradually become disillusioned and disenchanted. And in the end, the political authority would not even be a government of the people.

It shows that to develop a healthy democracy, it would have to be a step-by-step process for developing countries. It can neither be arbitrarily implemented anywhere and under any circumstances, nor can it be hastily implemented without being sensitive to the institutional sophistication or people's sophistication required at every stage of development. In recent history, we have seen the hasty adoption of "government by the people" in some developing countries that has resulted in buying voters, fixing the ballot, deception and fraud at election campaigns, and even killing of opponents. Then there are the nonperformance and corruption of the elected and inability to depose the corrupt officials even with extreme popular dissatisfaction.

China today does not yet have a government by the people in the strict sense of the word, though more and more people's representatives in the National People's Congress are making positive contributions in liaising between the government and the people at the grassroot level. The government is using the Internet as a direct communication channel to know more of the interests and needs of the people. So, what we see is that China is now a "government for the people" developing rapidly in many directions. After economic reforms have got to a certain stage, political reforms and cultural re-examination are put on the agenda. Recently, the government is explicitly encouraging people's participation in political process at the grassroot level to get accustomed to their rights and to familiarize themselves with the mechanism of village-type democracy. Gradually, there will be a growing number of educated and more informed middle-income people emerging who want more transparency, accountability, and their representation in the government. Eventually, some would feel responsible to participate directly in the political process. The case in China is also a direct rebuttal to the saying that democracy has to be forced upon from outside. The whole process described above could be a step-by-step natural internal process within Asia, however slow it might be.

Would China ever have a government by the people with the people electing the governing body directly? Not right away, but I envisage it possible, sometime down the road, though it might not be exactly similar to the Western paradigm of democratic process.

Aside from the cultural and historical differences, for example, the mechanism of the process cannot be the same for countries with a 40 million population, a 400 million population, and a 1.4 billion population. When all the major elements of the present ruling party have a similar concept of personhood, similar cultural identity, similar historical perspective, and other basic social values, then and not until then could I see it possible to have elections between two major subgroups within the party to check and balance each other's policies and effectiveness of administration. Actually, in Anglo-American politics, the two major parties are so alike in their world views, basic social values, and political philosophies that they could easily be considered as one party in Asia. They only differ in public policies, whether to protect the interests of the supply side (big businesses) or the demand side (consumers) of the economy, and in social debates that would not upset the basic political structure of the country to create social turmoil. It is a well-known fact that Anglo-American politics are the most stable politics in the contemporary world, despite occasional economic slowdowns and social disturbances. That is so, because the similarities stated above could provide the continuity throughout the different levels of administration, and across the different spheres of the political, legal, and military structures after a change of administration. An Asian example, in a small way, was when Hong Kong reverted from British colonial rule to Chinese sovereignty in 1997. It was very smooth, because the handover was under the principle of "One Country Two systems". After the handover, the previous political philosophies and basic social values did not change; the socioeconomic, political, and legal system did not change; and the public servants in the administration and law enforcing community did not change. Likewise, we can imagine how smooth the administrative handover could be in China if we had two subparties within the present party having similar concepts of personhood, cultural identity, historical perspective, and other basic political and social values.

On the other hand, when there were elections among parties having very different basic social values and political philosophies, confusion would certainly break out to make governing not effective and inefficient. For example, because Italy had political parties of very different philosophies bidding for power, it had frequent government turnover since 1945. With the Italian People's Party, Communists Renewal, Socialists, Social Democratic, Republican, Liberal, Greens, the Italian Renewal, and the Christian Democrats bidding for power, Italy had five governments in just 6 years between 1996 and 2001.[48] We can imagine the difficulties and confusions that had been caused. In worse cases like Taiwan, where if one party gets elected it would have one name and one flag for the territory, and another would have another name and flag for the territory. If the changing of names and flags is legally complicated, then through textbooks in schools, one elected party would get generations of young people to adopt one set of historical and cultural identities and another elected party to another set of historical and cultural identities, thereby splitting the national psyche. The undesirability is then obvious.

Realistically speaking, aside from Athenian small village-type democracies (there are village-type democracies already being practised in China), any democracy in a country of size needs not only the competing parties having very similar basic beliefs, but also sophisticated social and legal structures, as well as an informed and responsible electoral public. As John Rawls insisted, the minimum threshold condition for the priority of justice and a democratic society is that "a society must have achieved a level of wealth sufficient to maintain a legal system with courts, police and so on that can protect the basic liberties of the citizens, and government officials to obey the rule of law ... citizens must be able to engage in meaningful formation of life plan; e.g. media, public forum, school etc. and leisure to reflect on plans".[49]

In conclusion, democracy as a political institution is very important to all contemporary modern states, because, in a rational,

---

[48] See *U.S. Department of State Website* on Italy.

[49] See Robert S. Taylor, "Rawls's Defense of the Priority of Liberty: A Kantian Reconstruction" in *Philosophy of Public Affairs Summer* 2003, Vol. 31, No. 3, p. 262ff.

systematic, legal, and orderly way, it implements the concept of "the mandate of people" in the political sphere of a society. But we have to see, at the same time, that Western democracy contains many values derived from Western individualism which might not be suitable to countries in Asia. We need to acclimatize democracy with deep-seated and most cherished indigenous cultural values in order for it to survive the test of history. Therefore, where the soil is not suitable to the plant of individualism, we need to find or cultivate a particular variety of democratic plant that is friendly to the native soil. And we should allow that plant to be acclimated slowly before expecting it to bloom and flourish. That is the only way the plant will grow healthily and bear fruit and the only way the soil will benefit from the tillage of the plant. Any hasty growing of hostile plants in this soil without examining the nature of the plant will only lead to the plant shriveling and drying out; or worse yet, the hostile plant may suck up all the nutrients in the local soil, leaving it more barren and desolate than before.

Chapter

6

Law and Order

All that has been said hitherto in this book would come to nought without the assertions in this chapter. Talk about respect for the individual person, human rights, freedom, equality and democracy would all be mere empty wishes without the guarantee by law and without the government itself respecting the law it has instituted.

This sense of law, as I mentioned earlier in this book, is a unique and positive contribution of Western civilization. Law in this sense is not merely a governing tool for those in authority, but also a prevailing spirit and system of values and principles set in codes that are for everyone to respect and observe, including those in authority. Any society, no matter how primitive, would have a code of conducts and taboos. China, for instance, had very sophisticated laws as early as the Tang Dynasty (618–906 AD). The first emperor, Tang Gao Zhu, even codified the laws and administrative statutes in a form that remained unmodified till the 14th century, and it was said to be the basis of the first legal code of Vietnam, Korea, and Japan.[1] But the concept of law discussed here is different. It is a concept of law that overarches the lives of everyone in a society, including the lawmakers.

---

[1] J.A.G. Roberts, *A History of China*, Vol. I, p. 87.

Again, for instance, in ancient China, there was a debate between the Confucianists and the legalists.[2] The former believed that a society should be ruled according to people's conscience and the moral values that everyone originally has, but which has been tarnished by worldly debris. And it needs to be cleansed again through the teachings of Confucius and enforced by the personal example of those governing. And the latter believed that a society should be impartially ruled by a strict code of law, without any interference by human feelings. The concept of law in that debate is not what I will be dealing with here. In other words, the purpose of this book is not so much to examine the various concepts of law philosophically or judicially, as to discuss the most crucial function of law in a society as it tries to develop into a contemporary modern society, especially the function of what I term the "overarching" concept of law in a society. Also, this book cannot do justice to the immensely fervent discussions in recent decades on the nature of legal authority and social control as well as every aspect of social functions of laws, though I shall briefly touch on the modern historical development in the West to place my thinking in perspective. For instance, in the West, ever since the American realists in the 1930s started to examine the disparity between the legal process in practice and legal ideals, there have been lively debates on the nature of the legal authority residing in the hitherto solidly established liberal legal tradition, and its relations to the political authority and social milieu within which laws operate. In a sense, we cannot even talk about the nature of legal authority without mentioning some important milestones in that ongoing development. Let us first review the Western liberal legal tradition since, as I mentioned, this overarching concept of law is a positive contribution of Western civilization.

Any study of law in the Western tradition has to go back to the Greeks and Romans. The Greeks, according to Antony Alcock, had an ethos of the rule of law. They emphasized individual liberty of the citizens in the city-state situation, and had freedom of

---

[2] Feng Yaulan, *A Short History of Philosophy of China*, pp. 134–143.

thought and speech in intellectual inquiry. "A Greek was free not because he governed himself, but because he was governed by known laws which respected him and his rights".[3] In practical life however, a thinker like Socrates was sentenced to death for "impiety and corrupting the youths." A charge that, of course, he disageed, but he drank the hemlock as prescribed to end his life anyway, because he was an Athenian and had to respect and abide by the law. Moreover, Greek citizens had the right to elect representatives to the assembly, which adjudicated the affairs of the society. Also, the Twelve Tables of Law by the Greeks later formed the basis of Roman laws.[4] In many ways, according to Alcock, Roman law provided the fundamentals of justice in the Western world today. For example, they laid down:

> the principle that every citizen is equal before the law; that he or she must know the charge against him or her; that the accused has the right to defend himself or herself, or be defended at public expense if need be; that the burden of proof should lie with the plaintiff rather than the defendant; that people of unsound mind could not be held legally responsible for their actions; that there should be a statute of limitation (twenty years for criminal offences); that the notion of intent in the commission of a crime was important.[5]

And, Alcock continues, the Romans also laid down court procedures, comprehensive family laws, property laws, and *gave personality to corporations* in order to ensure continuity. The importance of that tradition is that there were not only concerns over citizens' rights and legal protection of their rights, but also legal procedures to process the laws.

This tradition was interrupted by the invasions of the "barbarians". There was not much secular intellectual activity during the Dark Ages in Europe. Centers of learning were limited to the monasteries of the Christian Church. From the 11th century to the

---

[3] *A Short History of Europe*, p. 3.

[4] See *Ibid*, p. 33.

[5] *Ibid*, pp. 34–35.

14th century, however, there were profound intellectual activities in the fields of Christian philosophy and theology. There was also much commercial activity as well as turmoil from the Crusaders' campaigns by the Christian Countries and counter campaigns by Islamic forces, but much of the intellectual activity in Europe revolved around expositions and apologies of the Christian faith, because they had no direct contact with the Greco-Roman culture. When some scholars, according to Alcock, before the end of the 14th century, moved to Italy before the Turks seized Constantinople, bringing with them Greek texts on thinkers like Plato and Aristotle, it made Europe rediscover antiquity, including the Greco-Roman legal tradition. There began a renaissance (a rebirth) of the civilization of antiquity in Europe, and a revival of humanistic enquiry, together with a confidence in reason.

Alcock notes that with new discoveries and advances in astronomy, like the works of Copernicus, Galileo, and Kepler; in mathematics, like the works of Napier and Descartes; in physics and mathematics, like the works of Boyle and Newton; the founding of learned societies in London and Paris between the middle of 16th till 18th century, Europe entered the period of Enlightenment in which people discovered the power of reason and wanted to understand everything by reason and empirical evidence. Parenthetically, together with this spirit, the Greco-Roman plus the Judeo-Christian traditions have often become known as the roots of Western culture when people refer to Western culture in general. In this milieu of Enlightenment, an important study of laws was published in 1748, Charles L.S. Montesquieu's book, *The Spirit of the Laws*. It was widely read at the time. Although John Locke in England and Samuel F. Pufendorf on the continent before Montesquieu dealt a great deal on laws concerning the authority of the monarch and liberty of the people, Montesquieu's study, in the emphasis of empirical evidence of the time, was novel in that it was trying to formulate a principle or spirit of laws from an extensive social survey of laws in different lands.

Montesquieu traveled extensively before he wrote *The Spirit of the Laws*. He later realized that in reality, many factors influenced the formation of laws in a particular society. Thus he wrote:

> Laws should be so appropriate to the people for whom they are made that it is very unlikely that the laws of one nation can suit another. Laws must relate to the principle of the government that is established or that one wants to establish, whether those laws form it as do political laws, or maintain it, as do civil laws. They should be related to the physical aspect of the country; to the climate; be it freezing, torrid or temperate; to the properties of the terrain; its location and extent; to the way of life of the people. be they plowmen, hunters or herdsmen; they should relate to the degree of liberty that the constitution can sustain, to the religion of the inhabitants, their inclination, their wealth, their number, their commerce, their mores and their manners; finally the laws are related to one another, to their origin, to the purpose of the legislator and to the order of things on which they are established.[6]

So, Jean-Paul Marrot, summarizing his view on Montesquieu, praised him as the greatest man that century had produced, owing to "his love for humanity", his "hatred for despotism", his "respect for the laws" and his "zeal for the public good".[7] The importance of Montesquieu at the time, according to David Carrithers, was that he "shifted the focus of political theory away from the attention on mainly the behavior of the individual ruler or members of the ruling class, and onto the broader question of the structure and principles of the underlying regime as well as the customs and manners supportive of each regime type".[8] In other words, he saw that Montesquieu transformed politics from a psychological to a sociological orientation, and hence launched the science of anthropology, sociology, and comparative politics.[9]

---

[6] *The Spirit of the Laws* Book I, Chap. 3, p. 311ff.

[7] Carrithers, Mosher and Roheed, *Montesquieu's Science of Politics*, p. 2.

[8] *Ibid*, p. 23.

[9] See *Ibid*, p. 23.

Montesquieu's work is particularly relevant to the concerns of developing countries discussed in this book, because he discussed the structure and principles of laws, as I intend to do in this book, from a sociological orientation. And also, he saw that laws of different countries had to be related to the unique physical, socioeconomic, and cultural conditions of that country, though he was not promoting relativism. Montesquieu, according to C.P. Courtney, saw ultimately at the base of the principles that people live by, not reason, but human instincts for peace, for feeding oneself, for attraction to the opposite sex, and in the basic laws of nature. Thus, as I also want to stress, natural law (or principles that are given naturally) should be the guide for human action. Finally, as I also intend to discuss in this book, Montesquieu insisted that laws of a land must have a judiciary insulated from both threats and favors. Parliamentary laws were not to be violated, even by the king, after his edicts had been registered and announced as laws by judges serving in the high court.[10]

Another historical strand that is very important to the Western legal tradition started with the Magna Carta of 1215. As C.H. Wu reminds us, King John had been reasonable in his earlier years of reign. But, in his later years, he became oppressive to the extent that the barons could no longer tolerate the situation, so they forced the king to sign a charter granting them franchise. The charter gave power to the 25 barons to seize the king's land, if he should infringe their rights. That meant, for the first time in European history, the king was also under the jurisdiction of the law he agreed to institute.[11] This charter, together with the Bill of Rights in 1689, laid the foundation for the English constitution and the power of the English parliamentary system — thereby the "overarching" authority of English laws. We see, then, from the Greeks onward in Western civilization, a crucial development in European society was the legal guarantee and protection of the citizens by law, and the concept of universal respect for law, including respect from the law giving

---

[10] See David Carrithers, "Legacy of the Spirit" in *Ibid*, p. 25.
[11] See C. H. Wu, *Fountain of Justice*, p. 67.

authorities. Thus, according to John Finnis, laws in a society are to resolve problems in a community for the common good with a "minimization of arbitrariness, and maintenance of a quality of reciprocity between the subjects of the law both amongst themselves and in their relations with the lawful authorities".[12] And elsewhere, on the rule of law, Finnis emphasizes that the very idea of a constitutional government "…is the holding of the rulers to their side of the relationship of reciprocity, in which the claims of authority are respected on condition that authority respects the claim of common good (of which a fundamental component is respect for the equal right of all to respectful consideration…)".[13]

Of course, this Western liberal legal tradition philosophically, goes back to Locke, Hume, Spinoza, Rousseau, and Kant. All of them had to deal with the question of the authority of the laws without referring to the sovereign power of the country. Hence, all the contemporary theorists on law, whether they be proponents of positivist theory like H.L.A. Hart, political liberal theory like John Rawls, utilitarian theory like followers of John Stuart Mill, the natural law theory like John Finnis or the integrated theory like Ronald Dworkin, they all agree ultimately, that laws must have sovereignty over people to be effective.

A nagging question in a democratic society is how legislation could have sovereign power over people in the society, including the governing authority, while there is no sovereign power in the society beyond the governing authority to sanction it. The different theories, mentioned above, all had different answers to this question. But ultimately, they all had to resort to some given values that they consider basic to all people. For instance, Hart, while insisting that the judiciary system only had to deal with the facts of rules — "primary rules" dealing with direct commands or orders on conducts, and "secondary rules" dealing with complex procedures of legislation — a judge finally has to interpret the constitution or

---

[12] *Natural Law and Natural Rights*, p. 277.
[13] *Ibid*, p. 272.

decide on the standards of validity to adjudicate the cases. Thus, Hart says: "At any given moment, judges, even those of a supreme court, are part of a system the rules of which are determinate enough at the center to supply standards of correct judicial decision".[14] It shows that even to the positivists, the judges in English tradition have to rely on parliamentary customs or legal precedence upon which to validate the "standards", and finally, they have to resort to some well-accepted and well-cherished values such as liberty and equality to confirm the validity of the standards or precedence.

Then for instance, to utilitarian theorists, they ultimately have to define what "happiness" is, if the government is to provide the greatest happiness to the largest number of people. And if maximizing happiness is minimizing pain, then they have to define "pain". It is certainly not merely physical pain. If it includes sorrow over the loss of one's entitlement, or indignation over some wrong suffered, one has to have some basic values to judge what one is entitled to, or whether the sorrow and indignation are justified or not. In other words, the basic views on happiness and pain are determined by some "given".

To Dworkin, for instance, equality is a given value:

> Equal concern is the sovereign virtue of the political community ... the distribution of wealth is the product of a legal order, a citizen's wealth massively depends on which law his community has enacted; not only its law governing ownership, theft, contract and tort, but also its welfare law, tax law, labor law, civil rights law, environmental regulation law, laws of practically everything else.[15]

It is an integrated concern of equality. And Dworkin wants to explain that equality is one of the starting points of an "original position" for that integrated concern. But it seems that he needs a deeper theory to explain why the original position has the features that it does, and why the people choose a particular principle of

---

[14] *The Concept of Law*, p. 145.
[15] *Sovereign Virtue*, p. 1.

vindication in that position. His theory would, then, depend on the adequacy of an interpretation of equality that supports it. So, Paul Gaffney sees Dworkin's thesis as a position in which all legal decisions must conform to the overall moral vision of the legal system. And, to him, Dworkin, in a sense, "advocates the natural law conviction that law is essentially related to objective moral principles. The moral principles that under-gird the legal institution both justify and challenge the standing law".[16]

I am not sure Dworkin would want to be classified as a natural law proponent. But my examination suggests that whatever legal theories we believe, ultimately, we have to reckon with a "given" in the human situation to base our moral values or choice. And those moral values or choice would be the basis of our legal considerations. In the end, all the above thinkers have to agree that, however they define or characterize those values or principles, the concepts of justice, equality and liberty are crucial to political laws in any democratic society, and those concepts are basic and need no more justification.

The above discussion leads us closer to a natural law position that also starts with a basic premise of the "common good" as mentioned in two of Finnis's statements, perhaps not necessarily with a Christian assumption. That is also why there is today a revived interest in the natural law theories, though not necessarily based on divine law. Hans Kelsen summarizes it this way:

> The natural law is characterized by the acceptance of norms that are immanent in nature, and thus by the acceptance of immanence of values constituted by such norm either in the reality of nature in general or in the nature of human beings in particular.... Nature in general or human nature in particular becomes the norm-making authority [of human conduct].[17]

In the Chinese tradition, some of the crucial Confucian moralities were likewise derived from basic human nature. For instance,

---

[16] Paul Gaffney, *Ronald Dworkin on Law as Integrity*, p. 3.

[17] "Foudation of the Natural Law Doctrine" in *Natural Law* John Finnis (ed.) Vol. I, p. 129.

Confucius' most famous follower, Mencius, said: "We all have a heart of compassion and, a heart of conscience, a heart of reverence and a heart of right and wrong...these are not external things we meld into us. They're part of us from the beginning, though we may not realize it".[18]

Lee Yearley sees crucial dissimilarities between the Christian theologian Thomas Aquinas (1225–1274) and Mencius in China. The former emphasizes the process of analysis and result; the latter on conventional social rules. Lee discovers, nevertheless, that both held certain principles of moral actions that are not "inferred", but "known immediately and intuitively". He cites the famous example Mencius gave about a young child at a well to illustrate his point of natural inclinations of human beings[19]:

> My reason for saying that no man is devoid of a heart sensitive to the suffering of others is this. Suppose a man were, all of a sudden, to see a young child on the verge of falling into a well. He would certainly be moved to compassion, not because he wished to win the praise of his fellow villagers or friends, nor yet because he dislikes the cry of the child.

One of the crucial criticisms of this natural law theory has been that logically one cannot move from "what is the nature of things" to "what people ought to do"; skipping from "is" to "ought" in moral theory. But with the basic human inclination that we are talking about, there is no movement between the inclination and the action. That is to say, the inclination would automatically elicit action. To use Mencius' illustration quoted above, it was understood that when the man saw the child almost falling into the well, he did not just feel compassion and stood there feeling sorry for the child and then decided to take action, but he dashed over immediately to save the child without thinking. The example I cited in Chapter 1 about a construction worker who dived into stormy ocean three times to save a drowning girl illustrates the same point.

---

[18] *Mencius*, translated by David Hinton, p. 202.
[19] See Lee Yearley, *Mencius and Aquinas*, pp. 49–63.

When Germain Grisez, Joseph Boyle, and John Finnis are defending the natural law theory on the "is" and "ought" issue, they also give an example:

> a girl hastening to the playground, chooses to stop to help an old man, who is confused and wandering in a busy street, simply because she intends his safety, not because she realizes her choice to be a moral obligation — a duty she has not yet grasped, although in the circumstances it would be objectively wrong for her to choose to go on to the playground.[20]

It is worth noting that Montesquieu pointed out a long time ago that while each society, because of its unique physical, socioeconomic and cultural conditions had its own set of concrete laws, most have a more universal rule of law in order that the freedom of its citizens would be protected. And at the base of the authority of the law was "security" which was the psychological dimension of human existence.[21] Indeed, there is nothing more basic to a person than a demand for security in human existence. And that "given" would provide one of the basic justifications to the fundamental values giving sovereignty over laws. The same could be said about "self-respect" and "the need to be cared for" as foundations for those fundamental values. This means that, for our discussion, in order for any constitutional laws in a society to function well, they must be supported by principles that come from values that grow out of the basic human existential state.

To elaborate more, the above discussions show that principles or values undergirding basic laws, like the constitutional laws in a society, must be based upon some basic yearnings and demands in human existence. Take freedom, for example: it is a desire so basic to our existence that we know it from the moment we are aware of our existence as a child. Parents never have to teach a child to demand freedom, but perhaps only to encourage the child to use his/her sense of freedom for creativity and innovation. If anything,

---

[20] "Practical Principles, Moral Truth, and Ultimate Ends", *Natural Law*, Vol. I, p. 277.
[21] *Montesquieu's Science of Politics*, p. 293.

parents might have to teach the child discretion on when to be free and when not to exert freedom. So, the demand for freedom is naturally endowed. We then can empathize with others having the same desire for freedom (educationalists have found that empathy is easily taught). Likewise, when you scold an older child in front of others, he/she would be extremely uncomfortable or annoyed, because you have made him/her shameful (lose self-respect) in front of others. Thus, self-respect is another rudimentary demand that does not have to be taught. Furthermore, with a rationality of reciprocity,[22] one can sense that others would also yearn for self-respect and a demand for freedom. That becomes the foundation for the concept of equality. Therefore, the concepts of respect for an individual person, freedom, and equality are all derived from the basic human existential experience, and do not need further justification other than introspection into our own existence and an exercise of reciprocity.

Perhaps, a little personal encounter can illuminate the above point further. For a period of time, our son's family lived next door to ours, and our son often came to visit us with his 6-year-old son after supper. Once, while they were there, our helper's three-year-old daughter also happened to be there that evening. That girl seemed to find comfort by sitting beside, or even snuggling up cozily to my chubby son on the sofa. After a while, his own son got jealous and wanted to squeeze into that comfortable position. That caused a skirmish between the two children, with the girl screaming and pushing as if to say, "I was here first!" Then the mother of the girl came out of the kitchen and spoke out, "What's the matter? That is his Daddy!" pointing to the boy. It was all the mother had to say (not shouting), and the little girl sheepishly backed away without whining or even pouting her lips. To be noticed is that the mother did not shout, and the girl did not resist or go away reluctantly. What went through her head was reciprocity thinking: "Because I love my Daddy, he should also be in a position to love his Daddy". It was marvelous to have witnessed that incident. Aside from the

---

[22] 推己及人.

fact that I would like to see that tremendously intelligent girl go to college, the incident showed beautifully how the process of reciprocity worked in human experience, through the action of a 3-year-old child.

Coming back to our discussion of the basic human existential situation, I have just shown that concepts like respect for the individual person, freedom, and equality are existentially crucial to all human beings. They are not particularly Western. They are basically human. Of course, that is why these and many more have been included in the various stages of United Nations' the human rights declarations. Understanding the universality of those foundational values undergirding all basic laws, we are able to see that laws could have sovereignty even without a sovereign monarch or emperor. And then one of the functions of law in a society is to guarantee and protect those human entitlements just discussed, irrespective of which society one lives in. Each country may have more to add according to its cultural identity, but those concepts discussed in each chapter of this book, understood in each own cultural context, seem to be the bare minimum foundational values for a society.

I have been discussing the sovereignty of law in relation to the Western liberal legal tradition. Beginning from the early 20th century, however, there were hosts of criticisms in the West leveled against the liberal legal tradition. Aside from its neglect of laws in relations to social factors (about which I shall deal momentarily), it has been criticized for its stand on values like justice and equality not representing what they really represent. Those criticisms were first leveled by Karl Marx against the whole system of capitalism. Then, his critique of the class biased legal system was picked up by legal debates. But the point to notice on the subject of basic human values undergirding laws is that Marx did not contest the justification of those values themselves, but only said that those in power legislated according to their own class interests, and the high-sounding principles did not come to represent justice and equality for everyone in the society as practiced in reality. According to Brian Burtch, Marx's criticism was that laws in the liberal tradition have become a "key ideological function in (mis)representing legal relations as equal for all and a source of progress and social betterment".[23] These critiques then turned people's attention to the social aspects of laws.

In the discussion of this chapter, I shall mention quite a bit about Marx, if not for any other reasons, but for his tremendous influence on recent discussions on social philosophy. As Brian Burtch puts it,

> The writings of Marx have had profound influence on the intellectual thoughts and political practices. In the early 1980s, Karl Marx was the most widely cited political philosopher discussed in social science references. His critique of Capitalism and its institutions has influenced social, economic and political policies throughout the world.[24]

Thus far, I have been dealing with law as a means of protecting the liberty of the individual person. That is the emphasis of the liberal tradition (self verses the state). But when we study the social aspect of laws, we find that one of the important legacies of Marx is the recognition that laws operate in an arena of powers in a society. For instance, Iris Young pointed out that even in well-developed countries where there are well-developed legal systems built upon such noble principles as liberty, equality and justice, there are still people being exploited, oppressed, victimized, marginalized, and made powerless.[25] Now, even thinkers who are not in sympathy with Marx's revolutionary ideas nor in agreement with his economic ideas agree that there are social, economic, and psychological factors influencing the formation of laws, and in turn the laws have social consequences. Thus, early in the last century, there was a wide spread consensus on the need for a study of the sociology of laws.

As mentioned, historically, one source of discontent with the liberal tradition came from the American realists in the 1930s that

---

[23] Brian Burtch, *The Sociology of Law*, p. 52.
[24] *Ibid*, p. 41.
[25] See Iris Young, *Justice and the Politics of Difference*, pp. 41–48.

wanted to examine the "failure of the legal process in operation to meet the legal ideals".[26] That dichotomy was what David Trubeck, later in 1977 called the dichotomy between "laws in books" and "laws in action".[27] To study this dichotomy, a fervent debate started. Alan Hunt considers the contemporary debate on legal theories really began with Roberto Unger in the mid-1970s. Unger emphasizes the conflict or tension between those two different modes of order (ideal and reality), but both need to co-exist within the contemporary legal order.[28] He also tries to combine two types of laws: interactive laws, allied to consensus theory which says that laws in a society are products of the resulting interactions of various social relations, and bureaucratic laws, allied to coercion theory which says that laws are instituted to constrain undesirable behaviors. As indeed, all contemporary legal theories occupy a position on the continuum between the polarities of "law as consensus" and "laws as coercion". Coming out of Unger's critique is the important critical legal studies (CLS).

According to Alan Hunt, "the emergence of Critical Legal Studies is the most important intellectual development in the field of legal studies since the rise of Realism".[29] Hunt goes on to summarize that CLS gives a systematic frontal critique of legal liberalism and of the whole tradition of Enlightenment which tried to offer a rational and consensual solution to the problem of social order. It sees that legal liberalism revolves around dualism between self and society, or between autonomy and community, whereas modern Marxists have found that in reality, it is not two sides of the dualism confronting each other as unchangeable entities, but the sides interacting with each other. In other words, Hunt says, due to the premise of legal liberalism being individualism, it stresses solely individual liberty from the tyranny of ruling authority and social constraints, whereas the Marxist tradition stresses the relationships of all forms of social

---

[26] See Alan Hunt, *Explorations of Law and Society*, pp. 65–66.

[27] *Ibid*, p. 65.

[28] See *Ibid*, p. 66.

[29] *Ibid*, p. 179.

entities, of which the self with the society is merely one. There are also dynamic interactions among various other forms of social relations; such as parents and children, the rich and the poor, the powerful and the powerless, etc. In the meantime, neo-Marxists have also shifted their focus from "economic relations to focus on political and cultural relations".[30] Of course, according to Hunt, not all members of the CLS movement are Marxists; but because its analysis of the relationship between the economic and the non-economic has been so important in Marxism, "the looming presence of Marx hangs over" the debates within the movement.[31]

The purpose of this book does not allow me to enter into the fine issues of the debates among different contemporary legal theories. What I would like to stress here is that, as an outcome of the debates, there evolves a deep concern for the social functions of laws. Brian Burtch, quoting Eugene Erlich, said even as early as 1913 in his *Fundamental Principles of the Sociology of Law*, "At the present as well as at any other time, the centre of gravity of legal development lies not in legislation, nor in juristic science, nor in judicial decision, but in society itself".[32] Today, after the CLS debates, we are much more aware of the many social factors influencing the formation of laws and the social consequence of laws in a society. And through the legacy of Marxism, we are also much more aware of the different powers working in a society.

As far as the critique of liberal legal theory is concerned, there is, however, a possibility for a dialogue between the liberals and the neo-Marxists recently. When the neo-Marxists today shifts their focus from the economic relation to political and cultural relations, one person stands out as an important spokesman for neo-Marxism, and that is Antonio Gramsci. Although he criticizes the economic version of Marxism that had become institutionalized and fossilized by the beginning of the 20th century, and his "ideology" has been made a complete and inflexible system of

---

[30] See *Ibid*, p. 145.
[31] See *Ibid*, p. 175.
[32] Brian Burtch, *The Sociology of Law*, p. 1.

thought, he still finds it necessary to have an ideology as a short-hand tool to represent a point of view. Gramsci's account of ideology is fivefold:

1. Focus should shift from the intellectual plane of philosophical systems to the formation of popular consciousness of common sense.
2. Less emphasis on ideology as an integral and coherent "system".
3. Ideological struggle not as a "Titanic struggle" between rival Weltanschauungen [world views], but as practical engagements about shifts and modifications in common sense.
4. Ideology as an active process that organizes issues.
5. For Marx, ideology blocked and distorted other thinking. For Gramsci, it provided a mechanism through which participation in social life was possible.[33]

In other words, Gramsci uses ideology not in a sense I have been previously using in this book, but as an intellectual tool convenient for dialogues. The significance of Gramsci's approach in contemporary theoretical discussion of law, according to Hunt, is that it has given a general parallel orientation between Marxists and the non-Marxists, both sharing the dichotomy between consent theory and coercion theory. This parallel development between the liberals' and the Marxists' approach to law makes dialogues possible.[34]

And through the dialogues in legal studies, it becomes clear that my inclination is toward a kind of legal pluralism, or what Alan Hunt calls the relational theory of law, which "... draws on a sociological model of analysis ... by insisting that the exploration of the internal inter-connectiveness between different forms of legal relations, it will provide insights into the role of law".[35] The advantage of this approach is that it recognizes both the important place of

---

[33] Alan Hunt, *Explorations of Law and Society*, p. 228.
[34] See *Ibid*, p. 75.
[35] *Ibid*, pp. 224–225.

liberal legal theory in its search for the universal human basis of law, and at the same time, it allows us to pursue the critical search for social functions of concrete laws. For example, an important thinker within the tradition of the CLS, David Trubeck, believes that, while recognizing the givenness of the dichotomy between ideal and reality and between consensus and coercion, the import thing is to start with ideals. He stresses that: "...a system must begin with ideals basic to our society.... I propose that we examine the law in terms of its contribution to these values...a legal order is not an end in itself. The system must be justified by its contribution to more fundamental social ideals".[36] That is precisely what I want to stress in this chapter: going back to some basic human values and also the fundamental social ideals within each country that are derived from its cultural identity. At the same time, laws must deal with all aspects of the society, including the conflict of various interests and conflict of various powers in the society, and not only with people's political liberty.

The new direction in the critical legal studies of law and society, with the impact of postmodernist thinking on the nature of legal and political authority, is continually challenging law and other social institutions. According to E. Coma, quoted by Brian Burtch, the studies are "moving toward a more holistic approach, incorporating key variables of social class, race, ethnicity and gender".[37] The new direction treats these variables as interactive factors in legal decision-making. All of these are illuminating to our understanding of the social functions of laws. Although it is very important that postmodernism in recent legal explorations has exposed many of the legal realities, including how power is enforced through legal socialization of law school, and how cultural imperialism of Western powers is being exported through international legal requirements, I personally take exception to the mininalistic solution to social authority of the postmodernists. To them, it seems that society as a whole would, in the end, have no social controls. The only social controls

---

[36] *Ibid*, p. 72.
[37] Brian Burtch, *The Sociology of Law*, p. 218.

left are with personal relations. But I feel that, for whatever ills there are in the conception and actual practice of legal authority, a society must have laws that address the fundamental social ideals of the society. I think the critical issue lies not in the laws themselves. If they are biased, they can be amended and revised. If the legal authority is biased, they can be replaced. Therefore, the critical issue lies not so much in the impossibility of having impartial legal authority or reliable social control, as in how to deal effectively with the various powers and social controls within a society.

In view of the fact that laws in a society are to protect people and properties, and maintain peace and order, they have a social function of dissipating conflicts and creating harmony. In Nicholas Timasheff's words, the function of laws in a society is for the express purpose of coordinating, regulating, and constraining people's and groups' behaviors in order to reach a "social equilibrium".[38] We have gained much from the insights given by the CLS and the discussions of the postmodernists in recent years. However, above and beyond all that, the most important insight seems to be that there are powers interacting within a society and that laws have to deal with those powers, be they political, economic or social. A society is not just the people, the buildings and roads, the social, economic and political institutions, it also has interacting forces with which the laws need to deal.

First, a society is a complex amalgamation of forces of different and often conflicting interests. Some of the conflicts may be due to personal differences in taste, opinion, age, or family background; some of them may due to differences in economic interests and social or political priorities. That is why we need moral principles with which people have internal constraints and mediating attitudes. Also, that is why we have laws and law courts to adjudicate the conflicting interests. If the law courts, or some mediating agents, cannot be trusted as honest and impartial, or their honesty and impartiality could not be checked in some way, how does a society settle conflicts of interest at all? That is, if difference of personal

---

[38] *An Introduction to the Sociology of Law*, "Introduction". by Javier Trevino, p. xxiii.

interests is the very cause of the conflicts, how can we rely on personal relations to settle the conflicts?

Second, a society is also a complex amalgamation of interacting and often conflicting powers. In other words, there may be instances where there can be a conflict of powers between two spheres of jurisdiction which require laws to deal with them. An example of conflicting powers competing for authority in Europe in the Middle Ages was those between church and state. Thus, Europe and America today have very specific laws to separate the spheres of influence between church and state. Moreover, to balance the various potentially conflicting powers in a society and to reach a social equilibrium is probably the most important social function of law in a society, because the conflicts might end up violent and devastating to people and social order.

We see that brute force is more powerful than the weak, so we need to have laws constraining brute force to protect the weak; the armed are more powerful than the unarmed, so we need to constrain the armed to protect the unarmed; the majority is more powerful than the minority, so we need to constrain the majority to protect the minority; the rich are more powerful than the poor, so we need to constrain the rich to protect the poor; the mob populace is more powerful than the governing few, so we need to have laws to constrain the mob to protect the governing few; the lawmakers and law-enforcing community are more powerful than the citizens, so we need to have laws constraining the lawmakers and law-enforcing community to protect the citizens. Laws, then, are needed to provide coordinating, regulating, and constraining pressures within elements of social structures to reach a balance of powers. In a developing country, therefore, aside from having laws fulfilling other functions, it is paramount to have laws to fulfill this function of balancing the conflicting powers in a society.

There might be cases in which it is difficult to change the situation, even though the class-biased nature of the existing laws has been exposed. But in searching for an ideal vision of laws in a society, we have to envisage a society in which all powers can be checked and balanced, otherwise there would not even be a prospect for social order. Furthermore, the very fact that the bias can be exposed and criticized, assumes a sociopolitical system that allows such grievances to be exposed, and is willing to listen to that criticism and is politically capable of addressing the problems.

Also it might be difficult for certain developing countries to institute what I call the overarching laws. Countries that are used to rule by warlords or military dictators, may hesitate to have laws constraining their own authoritarian power. But as discussed in previous chapters, whatever political system a country has, it cannot get away from the implied concept that the power of the ruling group is given by the people of that country. That, ultimately, is the only kind of legitimacy of a government that is significant. "A government of the people" is the bare minimum of any ruling group if it is going to stay in power. Of course, the ruling authority is always more powerful than the citizens, and does not have to give up its power. But if there were no laws to balance the powers between them, the citizens (the weaker one) would first silently acquiesce. If this state of affairs continues, the people would then have passive resentment, and then resentment turns into anger. Sooner or later it would explode. In which case, we can say that the ruling authority has lost the mandate of the people. That was what the concept of Mandate of Heaven was all about in traditional China.

I have discussed the fallacy of the liberal democratic view of law. Due to its foundation in individualism, it stresses too much on the political aspect of the self against the state, and neglects the social relations of law. But its contribution lies in its search for a universal basis of the sovereignty of law. From that search we have asserted the givenness of the human situation and the basis of the values behind the sovereignty of law. Marx's contribution lies in pointing out the social consequences of laws and the effect of social relations to laws, and their interactions. It has also pointed out the power structure of the society and its relationship to laws. All of these are not to overlook the role of the individual persons in relation to law.

The overarching law is important for a society, because it would protect and guarantee the good functioning of a society, and more importantly, it would protect and guarantee the rights, freedom, and equality of the people, and the functioning of democracy in that society. In all social and political discussions, satisfactory dealings with the interests and needs of the people are the ultimate center of concerns. In the very first chapter of the book, I talked about the respect for the individual person being crucial to a contemporary modern country. All the above discussions concerning the function of laws are precisely related to the well-being of the individual persons and the flourishing of the human spirit. Therefore, whether it is from the point of view of the government's responsibility toward its citizens in maintaining a social equilibrium, or from the point of view of citizens' responsibility toward the society in contributing to social order, the individual persons are at the base of the concerns. In other words, the most crucial issue of all in any discussion of law and order is in devising ways to develop the cultural, socioeconomic, and political spheres of a society in such a way that they would flourish the human spirit, protect the human entitlements, and retain the human dignity of the people. Without that fundamental respect for the individual persons, there would not even be a reason to talk about freedom and equality or human rights.

As we have seen in Chapter 1, this respect for the individual person does not necessarily imply a respect for an autonomous individual in the sense of Western individualism. It is a respect for an individual person who is inextricably bound to the community. So, when we talk about nurturing the human spirit or guaranteeing human entitlement, we cannot consider it without the community to which he/she belongs. It is interesting to note that Dworkin, speaking from a Western point of view today, also attaches critical importance to the community in relation to the individual person. He sees that community can be understood in four ways:

1. Community as the unit representing the majority of people in it.
2. Community as having distinct shared responsibilities with the people.
3. Community as something people need. It is an entity in its own right.

4.   Political community is not only independent, but also prior to individuals.

Dworkin endorses the fourth way of understanding community,[39] and sees the political community as an important aspect of the individual person. Thus, he says: "Citizens identify with their political community when they recognize that the community has a communal life, and that the success or failure of their lives is ethically dependent on the success or failure of that communal life".[40] With this understanding of the individual person, it means that enhancement of personhood also depends on the success or failure of the community which, to a large extent, depends on whether the function of law in that community is being implemented successfully or not.

This brings us to emphasize that, in order for laws to function well in a democratic society, they need the active involvement of the people in making their interests and needs known, and in participating in the political process. According to David Carrither, it is what Montesquieu meant by "a love of law and country".[41] Dworkin also stresses very strongly that to have successful functioning of laws in a democratic society, one of the prerequisites is that citizens have a responsibility to make the laws successful in that community.[42] In 1961, when John F. Kennedy, in his presidential inaugural address, challenged the American people by saying, "Ask not what the country can do for you, but what you can do for the country", it was, at the time, very fresh and idealistic to those raised with the concept of individualism. Actually, to people raised with the concept of personhood discussed in Chapter 1, what Kennedy said was taken for granted. For example, In China, it is just assumed that the citizens had a responsibility toward the community. As the saying

---

[39] See *Sovereign Virtue*, p. 212.

[40] *Ibid*, p. 231.

[41] David Carrither, "Democratic and Aristocratic Republic" in *Montesquieu's Science of Politics*, p. 120.

[42] See *Sovereign Virtue*, pp. 5–6.

goes, "The rise and fall of a country rests on the responsibility of every single person".[43] Of course, the government must be judicious in forming the laws with the citizens' concerns in mind and the resources and powers of the community must be distributed equally, and be efficient and effective in implementing the laws.

Popular involvement in the political process is important. The proviso is that there must be a sociopolitical and legal environment in which the people could have the guaranteed freedom and a sense of belonging to a harmonious society, such that they have the incentive to participate in the sociopolitical process. Therefore, the critical fundamentals are: While the success or failure of a society rests on its people's love of law and society and their active participation in the sociopolitical process, the people's love for the society and their incentive to participate rest on the successful functioning of laws in protecting their rights through balancing successfully the conflicting interests and powers in that society.

---

[43] 天下兴亡, 匹夫有责.

Chapter

7

Concluding Remarks: Further Application to China

As mentioned in the introduction of the book, this is basically a methodological discussion on the intellectual foundation for development in emerging societies. It is not so naïve as to think that many global events are played out by world powers without geopolitical considerations and thier politico-eceonomic self-interests. Despite that awareness, however, it stresses that to think through some socio-economic-political and legal concepts important for developing system in thier nation building is likewise, important. It is of further importance for them to evaluate those understandings and apply them to development according to their own unique historical and cultural identity with their particular rights and reponsibilities in the global community. Otherwise, one would not have an intellectual refrerence to evaluate what to pursue and what not to pursue on that way to development.

Readers may also remember that I have indicated in the beginning that, except in relation to other general categories, I am using the word "culture" not to indicate the complete range of mental and physical activities of a people. Neither am I using it to indicate a special sphere of activities like those of the literary, the musical, and the visual arts, though I am extremely aware of the importance of this sphere of activities and their contribution to development, for people in these activities are some of the most sensitive groups in a society, and are usually at the forefront in experimenting with, and expressing creative visions, ideas and feelings through words, sounds, images, and movements.

I have rather used culture as the most deep-seated and cherished values in the heritage of a people, both ancient and more recent times. And I also made a distinction between cultural values and institutions values, traditions and habits in the history of a people. The latter three represent ideas and behaviors that reflect beliefs and sentiments of a particular historical period, and may not survive the critical test of historical challenges. The "culture identity" I have been using means the identity with the deep-seated and most cherished values in a culture that have embraced the myths, legends, narratives, the symbols, and the psyche of a people's history that the people of that culture are deeply proud of. For instance, in the Chinese heritage, the myth of the dragon with the accent on nobility, vigor and vitality; the legend of the public spirited emperor Xia Yu (夏禹) who, for the safety of the community and in diverting water from a historic gigantic flood, passed by his own house three times in years without entering it; the fable of the foolish old man who, due to his tenacity, could moved the mountain that blocked his way; the poets' spirit of spontaneity; and the artists' unconstrained free-flowing splash-ink paintings; symbols of pine trees, bamboos, and winter plum flowers representing ever vitality, unbreakable resilience, and endurance against severity respectively; the many narratives on such figures as Guan Gong (关公) who risked his life for the sake of righteousness; or the flute player beside a well-traveled road who smashed his flute when he heard the only person amidst all the passersby who wept after hearing his music (知音) had died; or the figure of Confucius and later, Mencius, who went from kingdom to kingdom to persuade the kings to rule by benevolence instead of ruthlessness; then the ancient ideal of harmony in equality through an imaginary scene as depicted in "Li Yun" in *The Book of Poetry*. There are also stories such as the Butterfly Lovers who searched for freedom in youthful love despite taboos; and the prevalent Buddhist tradition of the Bodhisattvas who, for the sake of compassion to humanity, renounced their own ultimate state and stayed behind to help those suffering from frustrations and pains; these and many more were all imprinted in Chinese people's subconsciousness through family and communal education. For the Chinese, these embrace the deep-seated and most cherished values that the Chinese have to uncover and identify as resources to evaluate the concepts that are prevalently considered important to development, be it in relation to the concept of person-hood, human rights, freedom, equality, democracy, or the rule of law. And these are the cultural identities that the Chinese have to use to evaluate the outcome of their decisions in development.

Therefore, this book, instead of joining debates by schools of thoughts on various topics, is basically to suggest a two-prong methodological approach. On the one hand, it calls for a serious analysis of the concepts important for development as I have done briefly in each chapter. And on the other hand it calls for a search for one's cultural identity. In this approach, I hold both a universalistic view and an identity-specific view: universalistic in the sense that I see the concepts discussed in each chapter as nominally important to all countries; identity-specific in the sense that we need to use our cultural identities to understand them and evaluate their implementa-tion. In this process, one may discover that a particular cultural under-standing of a concept different from a usual understanding could maintain the spirit of the concept and yet is more applicable to one's culture; or one may discover that a certain aspect of a concept that has been discarded and buried in one's history could be significant to the contemporary world; or one may find a certain aspect of a con-cept more important to one's society than other aspects at a particular time; or one may find that an important concept that was never pres-ent in one's cultural heritage, is yet very important for a contemporary modern society. This analytical exercise of the concepts and the exer-cise of probing into one's own cultural heritage are both extremely important for the intellectual foundation of developing countries.

In other words, we must try to dissect and understand the vari-ous subtle meanings of the concepts at more than face value, and try to understand them with one's cultural identity in order for the development to have the support of the general population behind it to generate an *esprit de corps* and a momentum for development. This is especially vital today amidst the influence of the kaleidoscopic thrusts of ideas and power plays brought by globalization. Without the awareness of one's own cultural identity, all the baffling concepts and undercurrent forces in today's world would invariably bring about intellectual and spiritual confusions. Today, even a developed nation, when its foreign policies have lost its deep-seated and most cherished values, would lose the domestic *esprit de corps*, the international image of greatness, and the momentum for internal growth.

A cultural discussion in general covers a tremendously large area of studies, and the topic of culture in the sense that I am using here is also a gigantic topic. The reason I have the audacity to venture into such an endeavor in a cursory way is that I sense something exciting and challenging, not only socioeconomically, but also intellectually, is taking place and from which something extremely important is going to evolve. At this stage, we cannot afford to spend too much time fine-tuning, but can only sketch a few rough outlines to depict the scene and encourage those concerned to take part in the conversations. Ronald Niezen also senses the same by saying: "...I, like many others, sense that something new on a grand scale, is happening in the world that requires understanding, which can only be approached by sacrificing some fine-grained analysis in favor of wider scope and a more ambitious conceptual structure".[1] This is why, even though I can only touch the surface of the topic like a dragonfly skipping over water,[2] I still feel it necessary to start the conversation. Detailed researches, discussions, and debates, which I am sure, will take years of attention from many scholars and interested people in each culture to deal.

---

[1] Ronald Niezen, *A World Beyond Differences: Cultural Identity in the Age of Globalization*, p. xi.

[2] 蜻蜓点水.

In this study, I started with the concept of personhood, because that concept's implication is far-reaching. The book shows that in developing countries, while respecting an individual person is important, it could be different from the understanding of Western individualism. Thus, while a person's rights and freedom are important, priority should be given to human rights instead of individual political rights, and to freedom from want, instead of freedom of choice. In understanding freedom, we see that, beside emancipation from constraint, there is also emancipation from poverty, which can be poverty of basic physical subsistence and also poverty of human dignity and human flourishing. It means that in the development of emerging societies, gaining freedom of social choice should be given higher priority and a much wider scope of attention than gaining freedom of political choice initially.

Concerning the need for cultural identity, the book shows that, to have really meaningful equality domestically, some aspects of it should come from legislation, but more importantly, it should also come from people's respect for each other despite their differences in gender, beliefs, and personal natural endowments (physical, intellectual, or emotional). In the area of socioeconomic and political status, respecting differences is not legitimizing their existing status, like the status of a particular class or caste, but rather a respect for the person as a legitimate member of humanity, and not his/her socioeconomic status. In fact, one of the characteristics of a contemporary modern society lies in its environment allowing for socioeconomic mobility, both vertically and horizontally.

Internationally, in the globalized world today, our discussion cannot stop at a country's border. The realization of equality calls for an extension of our domestic attitude to respect the differences in race, ethnicity, culture, and religion.

As a result of what has been discussed, cultural values should naturally be included in the definition and institution of democracy for a particular country, and its historical conditions should be taken into consideration for its implementation. It may have to be implemented in stages lasting a long period of time. Some people seem to think that, irrespective of local conditions, democracy can cure all ills. For instance, they would say a developing country has corruption, ineffective governance, or pollution problems, because it does not have a democratic government. But this book has taken pains to show that historical facts do not agree with those claims. At least two Asian countries that have had almost 60 years of Western-type democracy are unable to solve the dire plight of their people; and Russia that attempted Western-type democracy also nearly ended in bankruptcy 10 years later. There are, of course, successful democracies in Asia, but then there seems to be no necessary correlations between Western-type democracy and a successful society politically, socioeconomically and culturally. I have shown that Western democracy does not cure all ills, and even less is it an end in itself so that a developing country should pursue it at all cost.

Concerning social order, I have stressed that without the sense of universal respect for law, the talk of respect for the individual person, of freedom, human rights, equality, and democracy would all come to nought. Thus, even though this concept of law might not be in one's tradition, one should treasure that concept and embrace it. I can fully understand those who, having seen oppression, exploitation, victimization, marginalization, and the powerlessness of some people still existing in societies that profess freedom, equality, and justice in their legal systems, are disillusioned about the rationale of the Western liberal system of law and order. However, instead of discarding the whole concept of the rule of law, I think the solution is in trying to reform the legal system so that laws become not instruments of oppression of some on others, but that of emancipation of all members of that society, To do this, we need to realize that the reality of a society, among other things is an amalgamation of interests and powers, although its sometimes conflicting. It is precisely the function of laws to balance those conflicts based upon the ideals of that society to reach a social equilibrium. Those ideals come from its cultural identity. Therefore, social order has to rely on the universal respect for laws, instead of reducing social order by relying merely on the government heeding to the voices of small groups. Otherwise, the government will tend to be a broker seeking compromises among interests groups, instead of a government with ideals leading the people. Of course, a government must listen to the voices of small groups, and try to answer their unique interests and needs. But, we should never forget the insight of Reinhold Niebuhr given a long time ago that completely moral persons, when assimilated into a group, could become "selfish" and not so public-spirited in their outlook.[3] The history of the atomobile labor union in America is a good example. The union started out as a means of providing leverage to negotiate with the employer and to protect the rights of the laborers. But later when it got so powerful, its self-interest led to a negative impact on the economy. Its protection for employment led to resistance to technical innovations like robotic manufacturing and its continual demand for higher wages and benefits made American-made cars non-competitive against the onslaught of Japanese cars in the 1980s. Thus, it is not necessarily always wise to rely on compromises among small groups to achieve social order. Even though there are imperfections in existing laws and partiality in legal adjudication, the rule of law is the only instrument we have for social order. The conflict of interests and conflict of powers are facts of reality in any society, and will always be there. The function of laws in a society is precisely to deal with them, so there can be a balance of powers to reach a social equilibrium.

What history has taught us is that time waits for no one. Each developing country has to confront new situations and new challenges as it goes forward, whether one is ready or not. The experience of China has amply shown that it has gone through a long process of more than 100 years of torments, reforms, adjustments, wars, revolutions, and large-scale social experiments before finding its own initial solutions that could be described as a satisfactory, sustainable, and hopeful way of development, though there is still a lot of arduous work and a prolong search for cultural identity ahead in its journey. I hope that by learning from what China has gone through and will still traverse, other developing countries could have a shorter struggle and a less tortuous journey.

---

[3] Reinhold Niebuhr, *Moral Man and Immoral Society*.

History has also taught us many other things. One is, any exclusive emphasis of a closed and socially pervasive ideology in a society, be it political, economic, or religious, and any fossilized intellectual sociopolitical system without flexibility are extremely unhealthy for a society. Secondly, human nature might be basically good, but due to whatever reasons, selfishness and frailty sometimes tend to corrupt human character when given the power to do things unconstrained. A realistic view of human nature is that it is weak before temptations, especially the temptation of power. This fact we cannot overlook in choosing the type of political institutions in development, because politics deals with power. Historically, there have been intelligent, noble, and courageous political figures, and benevolent rulers, but few social and political systems based upon an idealistic view of personhood could sustain successful government for a very long period of time. And just because of that, we can never rely on the expectation of a benevolent ruler, even though we hope to be governed by one. Therefore, it is not that we cannot assume the existence of human nobility, it is just that we cannot rely on human nobility for a healthy and a sustainable political system.

Toward the end of this book, I hope my readers would excuse me and allow me to have a private talk with my Chinese readers. Hitherto in this book, because of my limited knowledge of other cultures and traditions, I have been dealing mainly with methodology and general principles. Now I would like to venture into some applications of what I have said to the Chinese situation. I have emphasized a great deal on the importance of cultural identity, because that has to do with a healthy national psyche and a sense of historical continuity and historical destiny of a people. This is important for China today, because for the past 100 odd years and recent generations, many important values in Chinese heritage have been thrown away together with feudalism. When China embarks on market economy, many people begin to throw away Marxism. Although the government is still trying to underscore the importance of Marxism, many people, especially the younger generation, see it as an idea of the past. Consequently, among many Chinese people today, there is a vacuum in the intellectual world of the human spirit. Yet, it is precisely in this region of the human psyche that an understanding of the self in relation to its community and country, including its history and culture, is so profoundly important, even though we may not have conceived ourselves as having a sense of belonging, a perception of purpose, and a vision of destiny.

Of course, with the influence of postmodernism, there are many young–generation Chinese, for example the "New Age generation", who do not even trust any rational understanding of things. They feel that the world is too complex for them to understand rationally, and there are so many forces not in their control affecting their decisions such that they cannot be responsible for their actions. Consequently, they do not reflect upon what, how, and why things happen, or what and why they do the things they do. They only respond to their immediate feelings and desires. They dare to love and hate without asking why, though they do deeply care and love each other as if holding on to the only meaning of their existence.[4] This outlook, however, is only possible when one is young and without social responsibilities laid upon them. And indeed it is only possible when one can afford to be aloof from the mainstream society socially and economically. There have been many experimental communities historically, like the Owen Community at New Harmony, Indiana in the 19th century America (though with an entirely different philosophy), or any of the utopian communities in America in the 1970s, that have tried to opt out of what they consider the undesirable mainstream society to have their simple and congenial lifestyle. But, those communities were possible only when they presupposed a well-functioning bigger society providing socioeconomic and political stability. Moreover, within those communities, they would invariably lose their original purity when they get very large and have second and third generations growing up. Then, all the considerations of medical and educational problems, together with the problems of morals, and the problems of conflicting interests and

---

[4] For a discussion of the New Age culture in China, please see Xia Yue-lun, "A construct of the Western journey — Post modernism and the new age generation" in *Lectures at Beijing University*, Vol. 4, pp. 115–137.

conflicting powers would arise. Ultimately, they have to deal with rational planning, political authority, fair distribution of resources, social responsibilities, and personal morality like any mainstream society. In the end, the original enthusiasm and energy of the members would be dissipated due to disillusionment. That would eventually lead to the collapse of the communities, like many utopian communities before them. In other words, while an individual might be able to escape from the mainstream society to live a hermetic life, generations of people cannot escape it. They have to face the challenges of the society with all its complexities, ambiguities, and frustrating realities.

Parenthetically, when I talk about a sense of belonging, purpose, and a vision of destiny, I am not dealing with the religious sense of one's existence. That, I shall address briefly to clarify the difference in a moment. Sometimes even in our daily work, the disturbing questions of meaning and purpose of our work would, nevertheless, debilitate our concentration and energy. Of course, there is much to be said about scientists doing research just for the sake of curiosity, or an artist or musician creating just for the sake of beauty or virtuosity. We should remember that the technical breakthrough that made present-day computers (not adding machines) possible was the binomial mathematical system[5] which two mathematicians explored without any practical applications in mind at all. When the Dutch painter Pieter C. Mondrian (1872–1944) painted vertical and horizontal black lines with different bright color panels juxtaposed between the lines, he had no utility in mind either. He merely wanted to see whether he could paint anything beautiful with just straight lines with no curves, though that became an inspiration for many architectural façade designs in the 1950s and 1960s in America. Even though such scientists and artists might not have any social values in mind, they have intrinsic scientific or artistic values

---

[5] The numbering system we ordinarily have uses 10 as the base, while the binomial system uses 2 as the base. With a complex formula, the total binomial numbering system can be expressed by 1 and 0, which makes it possible for a computer machine to express numbers instantaneously in large volume calculations by giving an electronic pulse or no pulse.

that are the driving forces behind their efforts. However, this book, being a discussion on sociopolitical philosophy, I should emphasize on the driving force behind development of a society in general.

In many cases, when a scientist or scholar submerges himself/ herself in a research that would be an important contribution to humanity, an artist dedicates himself/herself to a creation of beauty that is a contribution to enrich the culture of a society and humanity, or when an industrialist/businessman commits his/her whole life to solving the problems of country-building, they know what they are doing, for whom they are working, and ultimately toward which end they are striving. Likewise, to a great many people, except those who having to work so hard for their subsistence that they do not even have the time or frame of mind to raise the above questions, finding meaning, purpose, and a direction of their work will very much be important issues to them. The young could evade those questions when they are young and have no social responsibilities. But when they have to work to pursue a career and support a family with plans for their child's education, those questions become prominent in overcoming the humdrum of their work. I suggest that it is precisely in such situations that the question of cultural identity, the question of how the work is related to the civil society and humanity, and to what valuable ends they are achieving, will loom large at the back of their minds.

Of course realistically, there will always be those who do not have such questions in mind. They just want to live a simple life. The difference between those who find their life pleasant despite annoying irks and material scarcity, and those who always find their life frustrating no matter how well-off they are materially, is most likely that the former group has found, or is living comfortably with their cultural identity, while the latter group is still searching for that identity.

Even the relatively small group of elite professionals, who have very demanding work schedules, but can financially afford to live a carefree and noncommittal life, may also have to ponder those questions. When the party is over, the crowd gone, the lights out, and all alone with the effects of alcohol subsided, they, too, would sometimes ask themselves, "What is this all about?" They may work very hard to accumulate wealth and material things, but they do not know why they have to work so hard for those things, because they do not even feel particularly comfortable with the things they have worked so hard for. From what they wear to the music they listen to to the people they are with, to the things that attract them, and to the definition of happiness and success, they may not be able to identify as anything they deeply care, unless they belong to a small minority who have been thoroughly educated to claim those things as significant. Nobody minds to be lonely or to work very hard, if they only know where all that is leading to. To answer that question, they need to see what is happening around their community, in their country, and around the world at large, which they see as significantly worthwhile for them to pursue. Ultimately, what is worthwhile, significant, and valuable are always related to, though not necessarily derived directly from, the deep-seated and most cherished values in one's culture. This is the importance of cultural identity for individuals. And obviously beyond the personal, what has more far-reaching effects on a society as a whole is the cultural identity undergirding the socioeconomic, political, and legal systems of the society.

What I have just discussed is close to having some kind of religious beliefs, but it is not quite the same. Having a cultural identity, and caring for one's country and the welfare of humanity can be appreciated and accepted publicly by anybody in the same culture, whereas religious beliefs constitute something very private. For example, what has been said about the search for cultural identity, sometimes after we have found a purpose, we may still feel that our inner strength and physical resources are not enough, making us unable to overcome a feeling of the finitude of human power to cope with the flux of the vicissitude of life. All of that would lead to a sense of transiency of existence and helplessness of personal efforts to lift ourselves out of that predicament, thus a feeling of "loss" (失落感). This is a religious feeling. The quest for something permanent and reliable to provide an all-embracing meaning to one's life is a religious quest. And historically, different religions have given different answers to that quest. Of course, this being a book on sociopolitical concepts and values, I shall restrict the discussion to humanistic terms.

Even in humanistic terms, as mentioned above, the question of meaning, purpose, and ultimate vision of our daily work will, nevertheless, be thrusted into our consciousness and encroach upon our lives. That is why we have to deal with it seriously. While a society may have one general vision, culture has many worthwhile values that could enrich the pursuit of many people in many fields of work for progress. Futhermore, there can be many practical ways to realize a certain value, some feasible, some not; some may conflict with other significant values, and some not. So, the need for cultural identity is not to deny an open and pluralistic society. For instance, the "spirit of perennial vitality" could be applied to the profession of teachers as well as to the profession of performing artists. The "spirit of resilience" can be applied to the pursuit of a scientist, as well as to an athlete. The "spirit of benevolence" can be applied to someone thousands of miles away as well as to one's sick parent. To work for the betterment of one's country or humanity, one can aim at different aspects and different levels of a society. Likewise, it applies to the work in the international order.

By the same token, the search for cultural identity should not turn into a movement for a fossilized ideology, be it political, economic, or religious. It is dangerous because events of history are unfolding ever-new pages with new scientific inventions, new technological innovations, and new socioeconomic and political encounters are bringing new challenges. And new lifestyles will evolve, bringing unfamiliar problems, unfamiliar miseries, and sufferings that need inventive solutions to meet the new-found challenges. For instance, who ever thought that the economic dynamism released by capitalism would lead to the exploitation of harmless people in a society domestically, and to colonialism and imperialism internationally? Who ever thought that the "invisible hand" of capitalism would have to be supplemented by government intervention on market forces, and lead to social safety nets in many countries? Who ever thought that the "Brave New World" of human achievements in science and technology at the end of the 19th century would bring about the horrible events of insanity and human sufferings of two world wars in the 20th century and many senseless regional wars in this century? Who ever thought that the international movement trying to save the exploited class of people in an industrial age would become fossilized and end in a whimper? And who ever thought that an informational technology leading to worldwide communication and financial capability that has brought the world ever closer and more interconnected through the dynamism of globalization would lead to a new kind of hegemony causing insecurity, worsened poverty, and worsened inequality among people in many parts of the underdeveloped and developing world? History has told us loudly that a closed system of thought and sociopolitical practice just cannot respond to the dynamic development of history.

Marxism was turned into a closed system of thought in the beginning of the 20th century, and that has been overtaken by new historical developments. But the astute social analysis, the indignation at inequality, and the passion for the oppressed people contained in Marxism still stand high in human intellectual history. As indicated in Chapter 6, we cannot even discuss sociopolitical theories nowadays without seeing the imprint of Marxism. With the challenge of current historical events, neo-Marxism has now branched out in two directions. Ronald Niezen summarizes it thus:

> One inspired largely by post-modernism, takes the shape of a Marx-inspired celebration of alternatives in which Marx's abiding concern with world history has been largely speculation about contours of post-revolutionary society, a society that Marx never really bothered himself about, at least not far beyond a concern with how it was to emerge from world capitalism. Another approach to Neo-Marxism sheds almost all speculations about revolutionary transition and draws instead from the ideas of human rights and the Enlightenment tradition of reason-based social reforms guiding principles of radical politics.[6]

My reading of contemporary Chinese history is that China is now taking the latter approach of neo-Marxism. Putting aside

---

[6] Ronald Niezen, *A World Beyond Differences*, p. 7.

whether China as a whole has been successful or not in implementing the central government's policies, it is quite evident that China's
development today has a definite concern and compassion for the
underprivileged and even marginalized people in the society, such
as the disabled, the migrant workers and their children, the plight of
people in the remote areas and, more recently, the lives, the rights,
and the means of production of the rural population. This is
extremely important for our understanding of China today.

Some seem to think that when China embarks on the market
economy, China is forsaking socialism and instituting capitalism.
The phrase, "Chinese-style market economy" is thought to be only a
façade for capitalism. People who think this way, as mentioned earlier, mistakenly think that the market economy is a fixed entity with
a fixed and unchangeable content, whereas in reality, its basic principles are a skeleton into which we must inject social values to
work in practice. We have seen in Chapter 3 that depending on the
values we inject into our constraints on freedom, we could have
very different results. For instance, capitalism contains, among others, the values of individualism, the logic of maximizing profit, and
maximizing accumulation. And the socialistic market economy
contains its values of social benefits, the indignation of injustice,
and compassion for the oppressed and the marginalized, etc.
People would say capitalism of the West also has social concerns,
like the anti-trust laws, the national labor laws, and social security
to protect the old people etc. It is true that social critique throughout history and incidents like the Great Depression of 1929 in
America have made capitalism in the West deviate from classical
capitalism, but it is still based on individualism and the logic of
maximizing profit and accumulation. China's market economy does
not have to be like that, though during the earlier periods after the
open-door policy, China's economy was more like classical capitalism. What China is doing today in social concern and special attention to the underprivileged is important for our understanding of
China, for, to a large extent, these concerns are intersections of
ancient values on equality with the legacies of Marxism in more
recent Chinese tradition.

Let us retrack. Please remember all studies of Marxism will tell us that although Marx was considered, together with Emile Durkheim (1858–1917), as the fathers of social sciences, he had his own creative contribution in social, economic, and political analyses. But he himself emphasized that he stood on the shoulders of those who came before him. The intellectual inspirations he drew from were the values of the Enlightenment, the philosophies of such German thinkers as Georg W. Hegel (1770–1831), and Ludwig Feuerbach (1804–1872), though he was critical of their thoughts for lacking a foundation for social action, and also various forms of socialism prevalent during his time. It is this intellectual background of Marxism that has tremendous possibility of intersecting with valuable Chinese cultural heritage to establish a new Chinese cultural identity. I mentioned in Chapter 1 that Confucianism was well-known and respected by the Enlightenment thinkers of the 17th and 18th centuries. Putting aside the debate on whether or not Confucianism ever contributed to the spirit of Enlightenment, at least it is a well-known historical fact that Confucian values were well respected by eminent thinkers like Voltaire (1694–1778) and others. Voltaire once wrote:

> "By what tragedy, perhaps a disgraceful one for the West, that one must go all the way to the Orient to find a simple Sage, without ostentation, without imposture, who taught men to live happily six hundred years before our common era [BC] when Northerners were still illiterate and when the Greeks were hardly beginning to take notice of wisdom? This Sage is Confucius, who as a disseminator of social values, never wanted to mislead or deceive the people. Has the world ever seen a more beautiful principle of conduct since Confucius?"[7]

Alexander Pope (1688–1744) and Dr Samuel Johnson (1709–1784) also had things to say about Confucius:

Superior and alone Confucius stood,
Who taught that useful science — to be good

— Pope

---

[7] Liu Wu-Chi, *Confucius: His Life and Time*, pre-text page.

His whole doctrine tends to the Propagation of Virtue, and the Restitution of Human Nature to its original Perfection

— Dr Johnson[8]

The most noteworthy Confucian value considered by the 17th and 18th century-thinkers was, however, the concept of equality through which one is not judged by his/her wealth or birth but by his/her ability. And irrespective of how we now consider the content of examination in modern eyes, or whether one should consider the examination method as the sole selection process for human resources, the examination system of China that started about 2000 years ago was an avenue through which anybody, even a peasant, could rise to the position of officialdom, and even to a position of a prime minister of China. At that time the standard criteria of selection in Europe was a person's birth and rank of nobility. It is a well-known fact that the examination system first inspired the British and then the Americans to establish their civil servant examination systems.[9] Therefore, even though we do not have to claim Chinese values as being the root of Enlightenment, it was certainly part of the spirit of Enlightenment influencing thinkers of the period. Please remember, as I mentioned in the Introduction, what caught the imagination of Chinese intellectuals about Marxism in the early 20th century was precisely the similarity between its passion for universal equality and the traditional Chinese ideal of equality and a world with Grand Harmony (大同世界).

So, when we talk about values in Chinese tradition as a whole, we should not only mean the ancient, but also the more recent Chinese heritage, including the tradition that has made China stand up tall after about 100 years of torment and tumult. For instance, today, it does not matter whether you are a Communist Party member or not, you as a Chinese cannot but remember that China has become what it is today, because there

---

[8] *Ibid*, pre-text page.
[9] H. G. Creel, *Confucius and the Chinese Way*, pp. 276–278 (concerning equality and the examination system).

were thousands of people with the passion and dedication for a noble cause of equality and national dignity who have shed blood and given their lives for China. Moreover, the successful completion of the famous Long March cannot but be considered as an epic event in Chinese history:[10] The straggly revolutionary army of around 86,000 men and women with only rifles on their back and straw sandals on their feet, defending themselves while manoeuvring forward with enemy airplanes above and machine gunfire behind, crossing torrential rivers, climbing snow-capped mountains, and traversing through marsh grasslands, to arrive at their destination with less than 4000 men and women. One has to ask, what made those men and women have the will and tenacity to complete the march at such odds? You may say that they did it for self-survival. That is beside the point. The pertinent question is: What was it that made them take that option to be among the group on the Long March in the first place, and except those who deserted on the way, what gave those remaining group the resilience to continue on to the very end? The emphasis here is not that young people today should "remember the bitterness of the past in order to appreciate the sweetness of today",[11] though that is indeed necessary as a reminder. What I am emphasizing here is that as far as the Chinese cultural identity is concerned, whatever ideals that had led the group of men and women to go on the Long March, the spirit behind that epic event of modern Chinese history should never be forgotten as part of the most cherished values of Chinese tradition.

---

[10] A ludicrous conjecture that the Long March was a "puppet-show" staged by Stalin and Chiang Kai-Shek, claimed by June Chang and Jon Halliday in their book, *Mao: the Unknown Story*, just cannot be taken seriously. For, among its voluminous notes from various archives and personal accounts, there is not a single word in them to substantiate their conjecture. What is revealed in the notes are all well-known historical facts, and their conjecture or what they considered as the "unknown" part of the story is nowhere verified by any document. For a more balanced account of the event, see *The Long March*, Jocelyn and Andrew McEwen (eds.).

[11] 忆苦思甜.

We have already seen the intersection of Chinese historical values with Marxist values. The contribution of neo-Marxism today is its analysis of social relations, its indignation at inequality, and its passion to strive on behalf of the oppressed people. Marx's famous words were: "The philosophers have only interpreted the world in various ways; the point however is to change it".[12] There have been many peasant rebellions in Chinese history to change things, but they were for self-survival under unbearable oppressions. The Chinese revolution led by Sun Yat-Sen to overthrow the Qing Dynasty and to establish a republic started and was put in force by political ideals, but its ideals did not awake the slumber of the general masses and obtain their support. What China has learned from Marxism is that when faced with injustice, one is not just to sigh and complain about the sad state of affairs, but to become emotionally indignant about it and to have a passion to doing something about it. The value of compassion is not foreign to the China heritage. But in Confucianism, it is to be conveyed through the policies of the emperor and in Moism (one of ancient Chinese schools of philosophy) or in Buddhism, it is more of a personal cultivation. Compassion in Marxism is a social value, calling for mass social action to change the undesirable situation. This is very much a part of the modern Chinese history, which we have to identify as a most cherished value in Chinese heritage.

Although we do not need to struggle with social turmoil for freedom and equality in today's China, we still need that emotional commitment and passionate indignation that drive actions to ameliorate seemingly unsurmountable problems. People in the West always seem to think that the only kind of struggle for freedom is that of the individuals against the state or the struggles of political dissidents. That is again individualism playing havoc, grouping all kinds of freedom under political freedom and grouping all forms of human rights under individual rights.

---

[12] Engels, *Ludwig Feuerbach and the Outcome of Classical German Philosophy*, p. 84, as quoted in Newton Stallknecht and Robert Brumbaugh, *The Spirit of Western Philosophy*, p. 403.

Nobody says China today has complete freedom of speech, and that everyone has complete political freedom. What needs to be said is that there are other more important considerations in the present stage of our history in development, just like in countries that profess the importance of political freedom, now also has to balance between liberty and social security, when faced with terrorism.

I have also taken pains to show in this book that there are many kinds of freedom, many aspects of human rights and different faces of equality. The lack of them all need attention to ameliorate. Even though China does not need tumultuous revolution today, there are many challenges that need people's compassion, dedication, and active participation to work with the state to overcome, and there is still ample room for ordinary citizens to make contributions in public services, as well as to do dedicated and conscientious work in one's profession or ordinary work. As indeed today, there are private individuals (some from Hong Kong, some from Mainland China, and some from foreign countries) giving medical, social, and educational services in remote areas of China. There are entrepreneurs investing in backward areas to provide employment to the population, and there are individuals making a big noise about the pollution and ecological problems in China. In any case, whether government officials or ordinary citizens, to be concerned with, and finding ways to tackle, those problems need a commitment and a compassion to meet and overcome the challenges. In this sense, university graduates going to the vast rural areas to improve the situations with their knowledge and training is not personal sacrifice, but just an employment opportunity, even for a short term. Thousands of university graduates trying to find employment each year just in the cities and leaving the opportunities in the bigger part of China's vast hinterland unconsidered, is definitely unhealthy for a country. It should be a new mission for the young people in China's development. Today, this effort should no longer be a political call for the intellectuals to be "re-educated by the farmers". A program like this should not be driven by a built-up enthusiasm for impossible ideals and absurd sacrifices without organization, because that invariably end in disillusionment and might even end in personal tragedies. It should be a personal decision to do something in the vast rural areas as an opportunity to live the cultural identity one has found, and to contribute one's knowledge and usefulness for China's development in various ways to deal with different needs of the country. We do not need to go to the most difficult places at first, because it is not a competition to see who is most courageous and most selfless. It is to participate in a reality of development to fulfill one of the missions of educated people in the rural areas. At first, the city graduates could go to the rural towns, those graduates coming from towns could go to the near by villages, and those from the villages could go to the more remote areas, until everyone is acclimated with the local conditions. Then, the city graduates could go further into the villages and more remote areas, even for a short period of 2 to 3 years initially. In other words, the whole endeavor should not be a sensational political movement, but a long-term realistic national strategy of socioeconomic and cultural development.

Of course, cultural values alone, or even a passion for putting important values into practice, are not enough for development, nor is it enough to have artistic creativity to enrich our imagination and broaden our horizon in suggesting possible visions, we also need the most up-to-date physical, biological, medical, and informational sciences and technologies, plus the economic, social, political, and legal sciences to inform, guide, and enable the government to plan, design, and overcome very difficult practical problems in executing developments. It is obvious, then, education has a tremendously important role to play here, even to prepare for the much-needed social and medical services. Thus, to bring the educated to meet the challenges of the vast areas needing the fruits of education is not hard to see as an important step in development. In this process, while informational data and knowledge can be transferred in a relatively short time, values, on the other hand, have to be nurtured through a much longer process. That is why education in cultural values are also important in rural areas. It is another area university graduates in the humanities could be useful.

But this, like establishing a rural public health system and building a physical infrastructure, it needs government's priority in funding. The urgency will always be prompted by what our cultural identity tells us is important and what should be prioritized.

China's rural problems, including the needs to improve the scope and quality of rural education, have been concerns of many people even as early as the latter part of the 19th century. But whatever pilot projects there were, they were by private institutions or private individuals, Chinese or foreign, without systematic backing from the government and thus, the scope was limited. Now, when the government engages itself in solving the rural problems, beside the consideration of expanding domestic purchasing power, it stems also from an indignation at the unacceptable situation in the rural areas and a compassion for those in their miserable plight. This is a concrete expression of the cultural identity from a recent Chinese heritage just mentioned.

Therefore, I see a convergence of three strands of cultural values in China today. At least what is evident today is that there are the Chinese ancient values, the Marxist social analysis and social compassion, and the contribution of Western liberalism like the universal respect for law, the modern practice of the skeleton of democratic process. They all seem to have intersected. That is, beside the physical sciences and the arts which are without national and cultural boundaries, I have a vision that these three important strands of cultural heritages will converge like the confluence of three torrential streams merging into a mighty roaring river. Could this be part of a picture delineating the often heard phrase: "Chinese-style Socialism?"

A word of caution to our younger Chinese generation: Although the Chinese leaders are very low-key in China's preliminary success today, I notice that there are some irrational conceit or arrogance expressed on the Internet by many Chinese people today. It is understandable that, after a century of humiliation that has made people unable to lift up their heads, and now when

China can finally stand up, you would naturally want to vent that pent-up feeling of disgust, disgrace, and unfairness. But, after gaining national confidence, I hope the Chinese populace would not forget the most cherished Chinese virtue of modesty, as indeed, China still has a lot of work to do. There is nothing to boast about. Even after China has become strong and successful, I still hope that we do not forget what history has taught us how great empires fell. The Roman Empire fell because of its arrogance in its invulnerability and indulgence in pleasure; the Qing dynasty of China fell because of its arrogance in thinking it was the center of the universe and in considering others as barbarians not to be taken seriously. Today, many of my American friends are worrying that America might also fall because of its arrogance in thinking that due to its technological and military might it is above all international laws and world opinions, choosing to forsake all the values that have made America great once upon a time.[13] So, I sincerely hope that the readers of this book would spread the most cherished Chinese virtue of modesty among the Chinese people. Of course, when the country is being threatened or the nation's sovereignty is being challenged, we naturally need to defend ourselves in whatever ways necessary. The famous dictum by Mao Zedong still applies: "If others do not provoke us, we would not provoke them. If others provoke us, we shall certainly fight back".[14] So, modesty is not humility without character. As the Chinese saying goes, "Conceited arrogance we should not have, yet integrity of character we should not have without".[15] That character in Chinese tradition is a person's stature built upon many values derived from our cultural identity. With these words, I hope my Chinese readers will dig more inwardly and boast less outwardly. This, of course does not mean that university students should be too humble about one's own ability and aspiration in applying for a job. That is the kind of stifling humility in traditional morality that we have to grow

---

[13] See Noam Chomsky, *The Failed States*.

[14] 人不犯我，我不犯人 人若犯我，我必犯人.

[15] 傲气不可有，骨气不可无.

out of. Boastfulness about oneself or one's country is arrogance beyond reality. To speak frankly and factually about oneself or one's country is not boastfulness.

This short excursion into a private talk with my Chinese readers is also an expression of my belief that no mighty river comes from one single source, but from the confluence of many small streams which again come from countless trickles of melting ice water from high mountains. I hope friends from various developing countries may find what was said in this book useful as food for thought, inspirational as subjects for conversations, and contributive as resources for meeting challenges of development in your own countries.

References

A Collection of Chinese Laws and Regulations to Guarantee Urban Ethnic Minorities' Rights and Interests, Beijing: Policy and Law Department, State Ethnic Affairs Commission (2000).

Alcock, Antony, *A Short History of Europe: From the Greeks and Romans to the Present Day Basinfstoke*, Hampshire: Macmillan Press Ltd. (1998).

Ames, Roger and Hall, David (trans.), *Daodejing : Making this Life Significant*, New York: Ballantine Books (2003).

Anshen, Ruth Nanda (ed.), *Freedom, Its Meaning*, London: Allen and Unwin (1942).

Asia Development Bank, *The Philippines*, Foreign Government Documents (2005).

Bacevich, Andrew J., *American Empire*, Cambridge, Mass: Harvard University Press (2002).

Beauvoir, Simone de, *The Long March: An Account of Modern China*, W. Austryn (trans.) London: Phoenix Press (2001).

Benesch, Walter and Wilson, Edwards, "Continuum logic: A Chinese contribution to knowledge and understanding in philosophy and science" *Journal of Chinese Philosophy*, December (2002).

Blum, William, *Killing Hope*, London: Zed Books (2003).

Brown, Robert and Gutterman, Alan (eds.), *Asia Economic and Legal Development: Uncertainty, Rrisk and Legal Efficiency*, London: Kluwar Law International (1998).

Burawoy, Michael, "Transition without Transformation: Russia's Involutionary Road to Capitalism" http:// sociology.berkeley.edu (1999).

Burtch, Brian, *The Sociology of Law: Critical Approaches to Social Control*, Canada: Thomson (Nelson) (2003).

Cameron, John and Ndhlovu, Tidings, "Cultural Influence of Economic Thought in India: Resistance of Diffusion of Neo-Classical Economics and the Principle of Hinduism" *Economic Political Weekly*, Vol. 6 Part 2 September (2001).

Carrithers, David W., Mosher, Michael A. and Rahe, Paul A (eds.), *Montesquieu's Science of Politics:Essays on the Spirit of Laws*, Oxford: Roman and Littlefield Publishing House Inc. (2001).

Chang, Ha-Joon, *Globalisation, Economic Development and the Role of the State*, London: Zed Books Ltd. (2003).

———, *Rethinking Development Economics*, London: Anthem Press (2003).

———, *Kicking Away the Ladder: Development Strategy in Historical Perspective*, London: Anthem Press (2003), reprinted (2006).

Chang, Ha-Joon, Palma, Gabriel and Whittaker, D. Hugh (eds.), *Financial Liberalization and the Asian Crisis*, London: Palgrave Publishers Ltd. (2001).

Chang, June and Halliday, Jon, *Mao: The Unknown Story*, New York: Alfred A. Knopf (2005).

Chomskey, Noam, *Deterring Democracy*, 2nd Edition, London: Vintage (1992).

———, *Failed States: The Abuse of Power and Assault on Democracy*, London: Hamish Hamilton (the Penguin Group) (2006).

Cohen, Stephen P., *India: Emerging Power*, Washington DC: Brooking Institute Press (2001).

Confucius, *Analects*, Ezra Pound (trans. and intro.), London: Peter Owen Ltd. New edition (1956).

Creel, H. G., *Confucius and the Chinese Way*, New York: Harper & Brothers (1949).

Christians, Thomas, *Philosophy and Democracy*, Oxford: Oxford University Press (2003).

Davine, Fiona and Waters, Mary C. (eds.), *Social Inequalities in Comparative Perspective*, Malden, MA: Blackwell Press (2004).

de Bary, William T. and Tu, Weiming, *Confucianism and Human Rights*, New York: Columbia University Press (1998).

de Bary, William T., *Asia Nobility and Civility: Ideal of Leadership and Common Good*, Cambridge, MA: Harvard University Press (2004).

Denello, Natalia and Squire, Lyn (eds.), *Globalization and Equality: Perspective from the Developing World*, Cheltenhum, Glos. UK: Edward Elgar (2005).

Deruberger, Robert F., De Woskin, Kenneth J., Goldstein, Steven M., Murphey, Rhoads, Whyte, Martin K. (eds.), *The Chinese: Adapting the Past and Facing the Future*, Ann Arbor, Michigan: The University of Michigan Press (1986) 4th Printing (1996).

Dieckhoff, Alain (ed.), *The Politics of Belonging, Nationalisma, Liberalism and Pluralism*, Lanham, MA: Lexington Books (2004).

Dowell-Jones, Mary, *Contextualizing the International Cevenant on Economic, Social and Cultural Rights: Assessing the Economic Deficit*, Leiden: Martinus Nijhoff Publishers (2004).

Dworkin, Ronald M., *Sovereign Virtue*, Cambridge, MA: Harvard University Press (2000).

———, (ed.), *The Philosophy of Law*, Oxford: Oxford University Press (1977).

Feng, Youlan (冯友兰), *A Short History of Chinese Philosophy* (中国哲学简史) Trans. from English by Tu Youguan (涂又光), Beijing: Beijing University Press (1996) 9th printing (2003).

Fischer, David Hackett, *Liberty and Freedom*, Oxford: Oxford University Press (2005).

Finnis, John, *Natural Law and Natural Rights*, Oxford: Clarendon Press, reprinted (1982).

Finnis, John (ed.), *Natural Law*, Vol. I, Aldershot: Dartmouth Publisher (1991).

Flatham, Richard E., *Freedom and Its Conditions: Discipline, Autonomy and Resistance*, New York: Routledge (2003).

Fleming, Jess, "Self and (in)Finitude: Embodiment and the Other" *Journal of Chinese Philosophy*, June (2002).

Frankel, Francine R., *India's Political Economy 1970–2000*, 2nd Edition, Oxford: Oxford University Press (2005).

Ganguly, Sumit and Devotta, Neil (ed.), *Understanding Contemporary India*, Boulder, Colorado: Lynne Rienner Publishers Inc (2003).

Harriss-White, Barbara and Janakarajan, S. (Directed studies), *Adjustment and Development: Agrarian Change, Markets and Social Welfare in South India (Summary of Findings)* Project No. 5686, Funded by ESCOR, Overseas Development Admin.

Harriss-White, Barbara, *India Working: Essays on Society and Economy*, Cambridge: Cambridge University Press (2003).

———, "Poverty and Capitalism" in *Economic and Political Weekly*, 1 April, 2006.

———, "Understanding Markets and Social-Political Institutions in Developing Economics" in *Rethinking Development Economics*, Chang Ha-Joon (ed.) London: Anthem Press (2003).

Harriss-White, Barbara (ed.), *Globalisation and Insecurity: Political, Economic and Physical Changes*, Houndmills, Basingstoke, Hampshire UK: Palgrave (2002).

Heer, Friederich, *The Intellectual History of Europe*, Johnathan Steinberg (trans. and intro.) London: Weidenfeld and Nicolson (1966).

Held, David and McGrew, Anthony (eds.), *The Global Transformations Reader*, 2nd Edition, Cambridge, UK: Polity Press (2003).

Hobbes, Thomas, *Leviathan*, Beijing: China Social Science Publishing House (1999) (reprinted from the English edition by Oxford University Press 1943).

Hu, Yaosu, *The Asian Crisis and the EU's Global Responsibilities*, London: Kogan Page Ltd. (1999).

Hume, David, *Political Essays*, Knud Haakonssen (ed.), Beijing: China University of Political Science and Law (2003).

Huntington, Samuel P., *The Clash of Civilizations and the Remaking of World Order*, UK: Simon and Schuster UK Ltd. (1997).

Hunt, Alan, *Explorations in Law and Society: Towards a Constitutive Theory of Law*, New York: Routledge (1993).

Isay, Gad C., "Qian Mu and the Modern Transformation of Filial Piety" *Journal of Chinese Philosophy*, September (2005).

Jacobs, Lesley A., *Pursuing Equal Opportunities: The Theory and Practice of Egalitarian Justice*, Cambridge, UK: Cambridge University Press (2004).

Jiang Bian Jia Cho (降边嘉措), "The Great Epic Poem of China" (中国的伟大史诗 – 格萨尔) *Lectures at Beijing University*, Vol. 9 (在北大听讲座) 第九辑 北京, 新世界出版社 (2002).

Kallen, Evelyn, *Social Inequality and Social Injustice: A Human Rights Perspective*, New York: Palgrave Mcmillan (2004).

Kateb, George, *Emerson and Self Reliance*, Lenham, MD.: Rowman & Littlefield Publishers (2000).

Kenny, Michael, *The Politics of Identity: Liberal Political Theory and the Dilemmas Differences*, Cambridge, UK: Polity (2004).

Ketcham, Ralph, *The Idea of Democracy in the Modern Era*, Lawrence, Kansas: University Press of Kansas (2004).

Khan, Mushtaq H., "Drivers of Corruption in Developing Countries: The limits of conventional Economic Analysis" *Annual World Bank Conference on Development: Economics, Europe 2003: Toward Pro-Poor Politics–Aid, Institution and Globalization*, N. Stern and Ivar Kolstad (eds.) (2004).

Kirkland, Russell, *Taoism: The Enduring Tradition*, New York: Routledge (2004).

Krishna, R. Gopal, *India: A Nation in Turmoil*, New Delhi: UBS Publisher's Distributor (2000).

Kunio, Yoshihara, *The Nation and Economic Growth: The Philippines and Thailand*, Kuala Lumpur: Oxford University Press (1994).

Levenson, Joseph, *Modern China: An Interpretive Anthology*, London: Collier-Macmillan Ltd. (1971).

Levine, David P. and Rizvi, S. Abu Turab, *Poverty, Work and Freedom: Political, Economic and the Moral Order*, Cambridge, UK: Cambridge University Press (2005).

Li, Honglei, "On Human Nature and Development in the Dao of Human Administration" in *Journal of Chinese Philosophy*, June (2003).

Li, Xiaobing and Pan, Zuohong, *Taiwan In the Twenty First Century*, New York: University Press of America Inc. (2003).

Lilla, Mark, Dworkin, Ronald, Silvers, Roberts (eds.), *The Legacy of Isaiah Berlin*, New York: New York Review Books (2001).

Liu, Wuchi, *Confucius: His Life and Time*, New York: Philosophical Library (1955).

Liu, Xiusheng and Ivanhoe, Philip (eds.), *Essays on the Moral Philosophy of Menzi*, Indianapolis: Hackett Publishing Co. (2002).

Locke, John, *Two Treatises of Government*, Peter Laslett (ed. with intro.& notes), New York: Hafner Publishing Co. (1956).

Mahajen, Gurpreet and Reifeld, Helmut (eds.), *The Public and the Private*, London: Sage Publications (2003).

Mao Zedong, *Selected Works of Mao Tse-Tung*, Vol. I, II, III, IV, Beijing: Foreign Language Press (1964–1977).

McEwen, Jocelyn, (ed). and McEwen, Andrew, *The Long March: The True Story Behind the Legendary Journey that Made Mao's China*, London: Constable & Robinson Ltd. (2006).

Mencius, *Meng-Tzu*, Hinton, David (trans.) Washington, DC: Counterpoint (1998).

———, *Meng Tzu,* rendition by Ezra Pound and translated by D.H. Gordon Book I, A private printing.

Milanovic, Branco, *World Apart: Measuring International and Global Inequality*, Princeton, NJ: Princeton University Press (2005).

Mill, John Stuart, *Utilitarianism and On Liberty*, Mary Warnock (ed.), Oxford: Blackwell Publishing (2003).

Montesquieu, Charles L. S., *The Spirit of The Laws*, first published 1748, Cambridge: Cambridge University Press (1989).

Mu, Ch'ien (钱穆), 中国历代政治得失 *(A Historical Overview of the Merits and Demerits of Chinese Political Structures)*, Hong Kong (1955).

———, 论语新解 *(A New Interpretation of the Analects)*, Hong Kong: New China Publishing Co. Ltd. (1963).

Munro, Donald J., *The Concept of Man in Contemporary China*, Ann Arbor: The Center for Chinese Studies, University of Michigan (1977) reprinted (2000).

Myrtle, Langley, *World Religion*, Oxford: Lion Press (1993).

Neville, Robert Cummings, *Boston Confucianism*, Albany: State New York University Press (2000).

Niebuhr, Reinhold, *Moral Man and Immoral Society*, New York: Charles Scribner (1932).

———, *The Children of Light and the Children of Darkness: A Vindication of Democracy and a Critique of its Traditional Defense*, New York: Charles Sribner's Sons (1944).

Niezen, Ronald, *A World Beyond Differences: Cultural Identity in the Age of Globalization*, Malden, Md. USA: Blackwell (2004).

Nigosian, S. A., *World Religion: A Historical Approach*, 3rd Ed, London: Macmillan Press (2000).

Odenberg, David S. and Chappell, Timothy (eds.), *Human Values: New Essays on Ethics and Natural Law*, New York: Palgrave Macmillan (2004).

Ottaway, Maria, *Democracy Challenged: The Rise of Semi-Authoritarianism*, Washington DC: Carnegie Endowment for International Peace (2003).

Pitson, A. E., *Hume's Philosophy of the Self*, London: Routledge Publishers (2000).

Popper, Karl R., *The Open Society and Its Enemies*, Princeton: Princeton University Press (1966).

Pufendorf, Samuel, *On the Duty of Man and Citizens According to Natural Law*, James Tully (ed.) and Michael Silverthorne (trans.), New York: Cambridge University Press (1991).

Roberts, J. A. G., *A History of China: Pre-History to c.1800*, Gloucestershire, UK: Alan Sutton Publishing Ltd. (1996).

Rawls, John, *A Theory of Justice*, Cambridge, MA: Harvard University Press (1999).

Ren, Jiyu, "Why Has the Influence of Confucianism and Daoist Though Been So Profound and So Long Lasting in China" *Contemporary Chinese Thought*, M. E. Sharpe (ed.) Vol. 30 No. 1.

Rittenberg, Sidney and Bennet, Amanda, *The Man Who Stayed Behind*, New York: Simon & Schuster (1993).

Rousseau, Jean-Jacques, *The Social Contract and Other Later Political Writings*, Victor Gourevitch (ed. & trans.), Beijing: China University of Political Science and Law (2003) (reprinted from Cambridge University Press 1997).

————, *Discourse on the Origin of Equality of Men*, Maurice Cranston (trans.) Penguin Classics.

Sarat, Austin (ed.), *The Blackwell Companion to Law and Society*, Oxford: Blackwell Publishing Ltd. (2004).

Sabine, George H., *A History of Political Theory*, New York: Henry Nolt and Company (1958).

Schaffler, Samuel, "Equality as the Virtue of Sovereign: A Reply to R. Dworkin" *Philosophy and Public Affairs*, Spring (2003).

————, "What is Egalitarianism" *Philosophy and Public Affairs*, Winter (2003).

Stallknecht, Newton P. and Brumbaugh, Robert S., *The Spirit of Western Philosophy*, New York: Longmans, Green and Co. (1950), reprinted (1958).

Stannard, David E., *American Holocaust: The Conquest of the New World*, New York: Oxford University Press (1992).

Tamney, Joseph B. and Chiang, Linda Hsueh-ling, *Modernization, Globalization and Confucianism in Chinese Societies*, Westport, CT: Praeger Publishers (2002).

Tang, Junyi (唐君毅), *The Spiritual Value of Chinese Culture* (中国文化之精神价值), Hong Kong: Zhen Zhong Books 正中书局 (1953).

Thompson, Laurence G., *Ta T'ung Shu: The One World Philosophy of K'ang Yu-Wei*, London: George Allen & Urwin Ltd. (1958).

Thoreau, Henry David, *Walden and Civil Disobedience*, Owen Thomas (ed.) New York: W.W. Norton & Co. Inc. (1966).

Timasheff, Nicholas S., *An Introduction to the Sociology of Law*, A. Javier Tevino (intro.), New Brunswick, NY: Transaction Publishers (2000).

Tocqueville, Alexis de, *Democracy in America and Two Essays on America*, Gerald E. Bevar (trans.), London: Penguin (2003).

Troeltsch, Ernst, *The Social Teaching of the Christian Churches*, Vol. I, 4th printing Olive Wyon (trans.), London: George Allen & Unwin Ltd. (1956).

Tu, Weiming and Tucker, Mary Evelyn (ed.), *Confucian Spirituality*, World Spirituality Series Vol. I, New York: The Crossroad Publishing Co. (2003).

Tu, Weiming, *Confucian Traditions in East Asian Modernity: Moral Education and Economic Culture in Japan and the Four Mini-Dragon*, Cambridge, MA: Harvard University Press (1996).

Tu, Weiming; Hejtmanek, Milan and Wachman, Alan (eds.), *Confucian World Observed: A Contemporary Discussion of Confucian Humanism in East Asia*, Honolulu, Hawaii: The East-West Center, University of Hawaii Press (1992).

Van Der Geest, William and Tränkmann, Beate (eds.), *Democracy, Human Rights and Economic Development: Conflict or Complement*, Brussels: European Institute for Asian Studies (1998).

Vogel, Ezra F., *Four Little Dragons: The Spread of Industrialization in East Asia*, Cambridge: Harvard University Press (1991).

Vogel, Ezra F., (ed.) *Living with China: US/China Relations in Twenty First Century*, New York: W. W. Norton (1997).

Wach, Joachim, *Sociology of Religion*, London: Kegan Paul, Trench, Truber & Co. Ltd. (1947).

Wang, Robin R. (ed.), *Chinese Philosophy: In an Era of Globalization*, Albany: State University of New York Press (2004).

Weber, Max, *The Protestant Ethic and the Spirit of Capitalism*, Talcott Parsons (trans.) New York: Charles Scribner's Sons, 5th Impression (1956).

Wee, Cecilia, "Descartes and Mencius on Self and Community" *Journal of Chinese Philosophy*, June (2002).

Wen, Ci (文池) (ed.), *Lectures at Beijing University*, Vol. 9 (在北大听讲座 – 第九辑), 北京: 新世界出版社 (2002).

Weinstock, Daneil M., "Citizenship and Pluralism" in *Blackwell Guide to Social and Political Philosophy*, Oxford: Blackwell Publishers Ltd. (2002).

Wilkinson, Richard G., *The Impact of Inequality: How to Make Sick Societies Healthier*, New York: New Press, distributed by W.W. Norton (2005).

William, Joseph A. and Wong, Christine P. W. (eds.), *A New Perspective on the Cultural Revolution*, Cambridge, MA: Harvard University Press (1991).

World Bank, *2005 World Development Indicators*, Table 2.5/Poverty.

Wu, Chinghsiung, *Fountain of Justice: A Study in the Natural Law*, London: Sheed and Ward (1959).

Wurfel, David, *Filipino Politics: Development and Decay*, Ithaca: Cornell University Press (1988).

Xia Xueluan (夏学銮), "The Origin, Development and Characteristics of Humanism in China" (中国人文精神的产生发展及特征) in *Lectures at Beijing University*, Vol. 5 (*在北 大听讲座* – 第五辑), 北京: 新世界出版社 (2002).

Xu Yuanchon (许渊冲), (trans.), *Bilingual Edition 300 Tang Po*, 北京: 高等教育出版社 (2000).

———, *Bilingual Edition 300 Song Lyrics*, 北京: 高等教育出版社 (2004).

Xu Youyu (徐友渔), "Western Studies of the Cultural Revolution" (西方对'文革'的研究) *Lectures at Beijing University*, Vol. 4 (在北大听讲座 – 第四辑), 北京: 新世界出版社 (2001).

Yao, Shujie, *Economic Growth, Income Distribution and Poverty Reduction in China Contemporary*, London: Routledge Curzon (2005).

Yearley, Lee H., *Mencius and Aquinas, Theories of Virtue and Conceptions of Courage*, Albany: State University of New York Press (1990).

Yin, Baoyun (尹保云) "Modernization and China's Economic Reform" in (现代化与中国经济改革) *Lectures at Beijing University*, Vol. 4 (在北大听讲座 – 第四辑), 北京: 新世界出版社 (2001).

———, *Universal Crisis of World Modernization: Experiences and Lessons from Studies of Twenty Some Countries* (现代化的通病: 二十多个国家和地区的经验与教训), 天津: 人民出版社 (1999).

———, *What is Modernization: A Study of Concepts and Models* (什么是现代化: 概念与范式的探讨), 北京: 人民出版社 (2001).

Young, Iris M., *Justice and the Politics of Difference*, Princeton: Princeton University Press (1990).

———, *Inclusion and Democracy*, Oxford: Oxford University Press (2000).

Yu, Yih-hsien, "Two Chinese Philosophers and Whitehead Encountered" in *Journal of Chinese Philosophy*, September, 2005.

Zhao, Suisheng (ed.), *China and Democracy: The Prospect for a Democratic China*, New York: Routlege (2000).

Zamora, Mario D., Baxter, Donald J. and Lawless, Robert (eds.), "Social Change in Modern Philippines: Perspective, Problems and Prospects" in *Anthropology* Carolyn G. Pool (gen. ed), Gerry C. William (assoc. ed.) Department of Anthropology, University of Oklahoma, Norman, Oklahoma, Vol. 19 Nos. 1 and 2, Fall (1978).

Index